TEACH YOURSELF BOOKS

# ASTRONOMY

# ASTRONOMY

**Patrick Moore**

TEACH YOURSELF BOOKS

# About the author

Patrick Moore has been interested in astronomy since the age of six, and has specialised in studies of the Moon. He has his private observatory at Selsey in Sussex, and since 1957 has presented the *Sky at Night* programme on BBC Television every four weeks.

For UK orders: please contact Bookpoint Ltd, 39 Milton Park, Abingdon, Oxon OX14 4TD. Telephone: (44) 01235 400414, Fax: (44) 01235 400454. Lines are open from 9.00 – 6.00, Monday to Saturday, with a 24 hour message answering service. Email address: orders@bookpoint.co.uk

For U.S.A. & Canada orders: please contact NTC/Contemporary Publishing, 4255 West Touhy Avenue, Lincolnwood, Illinois 60646–1975, U.S.A. Telephone: (847) 679 5500, Fax: (847) 679 2494.

Long-renowned as the authoritative source for self-guided learning – with more than 30 million copies sold worldwide – the *Teach Yourself* series includes over 200 titles in the fields of languages, crafts, hobbies, sports, and other leisure activities.

*British Library Cataloguing in Publication Data*

Moore, Patrick
    Astronomy
    I. Title
    522

*Library of Congress Catalog Card Number*: 94-68413

First published in UK 1995 by Hodder Headline Plc, 338 Euston Road, London NW1 3BH.

First published in US 1995 by NTC/Contemporary Publishing, 4255 West Touhy Avenue, Lincolnwood (Chicago), Illinois 60646 – 1975 U.S.A.

Typeset by Transet Ltd, Coventry, England.
Printed in England by Cox & Wyman Ltd, Reading, Berkshire.

| Impression number | 14 | 13 | 12 | 11 | 10 | 9 | 8 | 7 | 6 | 5 |
|---|---|---|---|---|---|---|---|---|---|---|
| Year | | 2004 | 2003 | 2002 | 2001 | | 2000 | | 1999 | |

# CONTENTS

# Acknowledgements

The Publishers would like to thank the following – for the use of their photographs in the colour section of this book: Plate 1, NASA; Plate 2, NASA; Plate 3, Russian Academy of Sciences; Plate 4, NASA; Plate 5, Commander H. R. Hatfield; Plate 6, Patrick Moore; Plate 7, NASA; Plate 8, Palomar Observatory; Plate 9, NASA; Plate 10, Palomar Observatory; Plate 11, NASA; Plate 12, Patrick Moore; Plate 13, Patrick Moore; for his line drawings: Paul Doherty; for the cover photograph: Royal Observatory Edinburgh/AATB/Science Photo Library.

# PREFACE

Astronomy is both the easiest and the most difficult of all the sciences. It is true that astronomical mathematics are highly complicated, but it is also true that anyone can take more than a passing interest in the sky; moreover, astronomy is still just about the only science in which the amateur can make valuable contributions. Amateur work is genuinely appreciated by professional astronomers, who in some fields rely upon it.

What I aim to do here is to give a general survey. No mathematical calculations are involved apart from simple addition, subtraction, multiplication and division; no previous knowledge is assumed, and neither is it necessary to have any equipment other than one's eyes. I do not set out to present a comprehensive guide to observing; other books do that. But if you follow what I have to say, I hope that you will feel inclined to take matters further. Astronomy is one of the best of all hobbies, because it can take up as much, or as little, of the time you have to spare.

So let us begin at the beginning.

# 1
# INTRODUCING ASTRONOMY

I would like to start with a clear statement: 'Everybody knows what astronomy is all about.' Unfortunately, this statement would not be true. Even today I still find many people who confuse astronomy with astrology, and expect me to be able to peer into the future, probably by using a crystal ball. Yet the two subjects could not possibly be more different. Astronomy is the science of the sky and all the objects in it, from the Sun and Moon through to the remote star-systems which are so far away that we see them as they used to be thousands of millions of years ago. Astrology, which attempts to link the stars with human character and destiny, is a relic of the past; it is totally without foundation, and the best that can be said of it is that it is fairly harmless so long as it is confined to seaside piers, circus tents and the columns of tabloid newspapers.

Having made this clear, it may be helpful to begin with a celestial roll-call. Obviously we must start with our Earth, which was once thought to be the most important body in the entire universe, but which we now know to be an insignificant planet moving round an insignificant star – the Sun. The distance between the Sun and the Earth is 93,000,000 miles, and it takes one year for the Earth to complete a full circuit: more precisely, 365.2 days. The Earth spins round once in approximately 24 hours, and is surrounded by a layer of atmosphere which extends upwards for several hundreds of miles even though most of it is concentrated at low levels.

At 93,000,000 miles from us the Sun seems a long way away, but in astronomy we have to deal with immense distances and vast spans of time. Nobody can really understand figures of this sort – certainly I have no proper appreciation of even one million miles – but we know that the values are correct, and we simply have to accept them.

Just as the Earth is an ordinary planet, so the Sun is an ordinary star. All the stars you can see on any clear night are themselves suns, some of them far larger, hotter and more luminous than ours. They appear so much smaller and dimmer only because they are so much further away. Represent the Earth–Sun distance by one inch, and the nearest star will be over four miles away. (*If Earth–Sun is 2.5 cm, the nearest star is about 7.5 km away.*) The Pole Star, which many people recognise (and about which I will have more to say in the next chapter) will have to be taken to a distance of 7000 miles. It is at least 6000 times more luminous than the Sun, and yet it seems by no means the most brilliant star in the night sky.

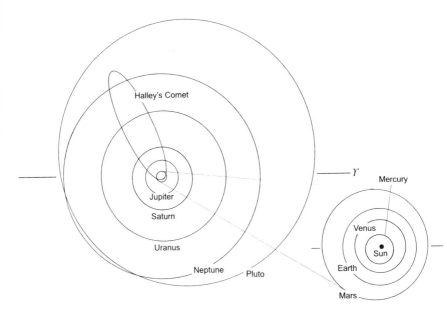

Plan of the Solar System, including Halley's Comet

Round the Sun move nine planets, of which the Earth comes third in order of distance. Mercury and Venus are closer to the Sun than we are; Mars, Jupiter, Saturn, Uranus, Neptune and Pluto are further away. Unlike the stars, planets have no light of their own, but shine only because they reflect the rays of the Sun. If some malevolent demon suddenly snatched the Sun out of the sky, the planets (and the Moon) would vanish from sight, though naturally the other stars would be unaffected.

The planets move round the Sun at different distances and in different periods. Even a casual glance at a plan of the Sun's family, or Solar System, shows that it is divided into two well-marked parts. First we have the four small planets (Mercury to Mars) and then a wide gap, followed by the four giants (Jupiter to Neptune) and one maverick dwarf, Pluto, which does not seem to fit into the general pattern, and may not be worthy of true planetary status. The wide gap between the paths or orbits of Mars and Jupiter is occupied by a swarm of very small worlds known variously as minor planets, planetoids and (more commonly) asteroids.

The revolution periods of the planets range from 88 days for Mercury out to almost 248 years for Pluto. They are very different sizes; Jupiter is over 89,000 miles in diameter, Mercury only just over 3000, while Pluto is smaller still. Because the planets are relatively near neighbours, some of them can look most imposing. Venus, Jupiter and Mars at its best are far brighter than any of the stars, while Saturn is prominent enough to be conspicuous, and Mercury can often be seen in the twilight or dawn sky. All these planets have been known since very ancient times, while the last three have been discovered much more recently: Uranus in 1781, Neptune in 1846 and Pluto in 1930. Uranus can just be seen with the naked eye if you know where to look for it, but to observe Neptune and Pluto you need optical aid.

What, then, of the Moon, which dominates the night sky just as the Sun is king of day? Officially the Moon is known as the Earth's satellite; it moves round us at a distance of less than a quarter of a million miles, and it is little more than 2000 miles across. Like the planets, it depends upon reflected sunlight. Obviously the Sun can illuminate only half of the Moon at any one time, and this is why we see the regular phases, or apparent changes of shape, from new to full; everything depends upon how much of the Moon's sunlit hemisphere is turned in our direction. It is an airless, waterless, lifeless world, but it is our faithful companion in space, and stays together with us in our never-ending journey round the Sun. It takes just over 27 days to complete one orbit of the Earth, though for reasons to be explained later the interval between one new moon and the next is not 27 days, but 29½ days.

Other planets have satellites of their own – as many as 18 in the case of Saturn – but in some ways the Earth–Moon system is unique, and it may be better to regard it as a double planet rather than as a planet and a satellite.

Among other members of the Sun's family are comets, which have been referred to as 'dirty snowballs'. They are flimsy, wraithlike things, and with even a major comet the only substantial part is the nucleus, made up of a mixture of ice and 'rubble' and seldom more than a few miles across. Like the planets, comets travel round the Sun, but whereas the orbits of the planets are almost circular those of the comets are, in most cases, very eccentric. When a comet nears the Sun, its ices begin to evaporate, and the comet may produce a gaseous head and a long tail; when the comet retreats once more into the cold depths of the Solar System, the head and tail disappear, leaving only the inert nucleus. The only bright comet to appear regularly is Halley's (named in honour of the second Astronomer Royal, Edmond Halley), which comes back every 76 years, and last paid a visit to the Sun in 1986. Really brilliant comets have much longer periods, so that we cannot predict them. Now and then a comet meets with a dramatic end, as in July 1994, when a comet known as Shoemaker–Levy 9 crashed to destruction upon the planet Jupiter.

Note that a comet moves well above the top of the Earth's air, and is a long way away, so that it does not seem to crawl quickly across the sky; if you see a shining object which is shifting perceptibly, it cannot be a comet.

As a comet travels, it leaves a trail of 'dust' behind it. If one of these dusty particles dashes into the upper atmosphere, it will have to push its way through against the air-particles, so that it will become heated by friction and will burn away in the streak of luminosity which we call a meteor or shooting-star. Therefore, a shooting-star has absolutely no connection with a real star; it is a tiny piece of debris, usually much smaller than a pin's head, which we see only during the last few seconds of its life before it burns away completely, ending its journey to the ground in the form of ultra-fine dust.

Larger bodies, not associated with comets, may survive the full drop without being burned away, and are then known as meteorites. Some of them may make craters; for example the Arizona Crater in the United States was certainly formed by an impact more than 20,000 years ago. Meteorites come from the asteroid belt, and in fact there is no difference between a large meteorite and a small asteroid; it is all a question of terminology. In recent years several tiny asteroids, much less than a mile across, have been known to pass by us at less than half the distance of the Moon. One of these cosmical midgets is believed to have been no more than thirty feet in diameter.

Apart from Pluto, the planets move round the Sun in very much the same plane, so that if we draw a plan of the Solar System on a flat piece of paper we are not very far wrong. This does not apply to the comets or asteroids, and indeed some comets move round the Sun in a 'wrong-way' or retrograde direction; Halley's Comet is one of these. In addition, there is a great deal of material spread thinly along the main plane of the system, which shows up when lit by the Sun and produces the lovely cone-shaped glow which we call the Zodiacal Light.

The planets were first identified because, unlike the stars, they shift in position from one night to another; indeed, the word 'planet' really means 'wanderer'. The stars are so remote that the individual or proper motions are very slight, and the star-patterns or constellations seem to remain to all intents and purposes unchanged over periods of many lifetimes. Board Dr Who's time machine and project yourself back to the age of William the Conqueror, or Julius Caesar, or even Homer: the constellation patterns will appear practically the same as they do now. It is only the members of the Solar System which move more obviously against the background, and even then the Sun, Moon and principal planets keep strictly to a band round the sky which we call the Zodiac.

The constellations which we use today have come down to us from the Greeks. The last great astronomer of Classical times, Ptolemy, gave a list of 48 constellations, all of which are still to be found on our maps even though their boundaries have been modified and new groups added. The Greek names (suitably Latinised) commemorate the mythological gods and heroes, together with living creatures and a few inanimate objects. Thus we have Orion (the Hunter), Hercules (the legendary hero), Ursa Major (the Great Bear), Taurus (the Bull) and others. Probably the best-known constellations visible from northern countries are the Great Bear and Orion, both of which are distinctive; the Bear never sets over Britain, though Orion is out of view during the summer because the Sun is too close to it in the sky. Yet it is important to remember that the constellation names and patterns mean nothing at all, because the individual stars are at very different distances from us.

Star distances are so great that ordinary units of measurement, such as the mile and the kilometre, are inconveniently short (just as it would be cumbersome to give the distances between London and New York in inches). Luckily, Nature has provided us with an alternative. Light does not move instantaneously; it flashes along at 186,000 miles per second, so that in a year it can cover approximately 5,880,000,000,000 or almost six million million miles. It is this distance which is termed the light-year. The nearest star to the Sun is over four light-years away; the Pole Star, 680 light-years; Rigel, the brilliant white star in Orion, about 900 light-years. It follows that once we pass beyond the Solar System, our view of the universe is bound to be very out of date. We see Rigel as it used to be 900 years ago, and if it were suddenly extinguished we would not know for another 900 years. On the other hand, light takes only 8.6 minutes to reach us from the Sun, and can leap from the Moon to the Earth in only a second and a quarter.

The essential fact is that the stars in any particular constellation are not genuinely associated with each other; they merely happen to lie in much the same direction as seen from Earth, so that we are dealing with nothing more significant than a line-of-sight effect. In Orion, for example, the two leading stars are the orange-red Betelgeux and the white Rigel. Betelgeux is 310 light-years away from us, Rigel 900, so that Rigel is much further away from Rigel than we are – and if we were observing from a different vantage point, Betelgeux and Rigel might well lie on opposite sides of the sky. In fact, a constellation name means absolutely nothing. Among early civilisations, the Chinese and the Egyptians had constellations of their own. If we had followed, say, the Egyptian system we would have had a Cat and a Hippopotamus instead of a Bear and a Bull, though, needless to say, the stars would have been exactly the same.

Naturally, this line-of-sight principle applies also to the wandering planets. When we say that, for example, Mars is 'in Taurus', what we mean is that the planet is seen against a background of totally unconnected stars which we happen to call the Bull, even though the stars in this particular group do not form any distinct pattern, and certainly do not conjure up the impression of a bull or any other creature.

But though the constellations do not change obviously over many centuries, they are not absolutely permanent. The stars are not fixed in space; they are rushing about in all sorts of directions at all sorts of speeds, and it is only their remoteness which makes them appear sluggish (just as a jet moving against the clouds will seem to move much more slowly than a sparrow flying around at tree-top level). Eventually the constellation patterns will change, and if we could come back in, say, 50,000 years, the night sky would seem very unfamiliar.

Our Sun is a member of a system which we call the Galaxy. It contains about 100,000 million stars altogether, arranged in a form which is usually likened to a double-convex lens but which I prefer to compare with the shape of two fried eggs clapped together back to back. The Sun, together with the Earth and other members of its family, lies not far from the main plane of the Galaxy, but is nowhere near the centre of the system, which is almost 30,000 light-years from us; the overall diameter of the Galaxy is of the order of 100,000 light-years. When we look along the main plane we see many stars in almost the same direction, and this is what produces the Milky Way, that lovely, glowing band which stretches across the night sky from one horizon to the other. The Milky Way is made up of stars, seemingly so close together that they are in danger of colliding with each other, but once again appearances are deceptive. The stars are widely spaced, and in average regions of the Galaxy, at least, direct collisions must be very rare indeed. Even 'close encounters' occur very seldom.

Here and there we find whole clusters of stars, some of them loose and irregular in form, others symmetrical and globular. Of the open clusters the most famous is that of the Pleiades or Seven Sisters, a familiar sight in the night sky from late autumn to early spring (in the northern hemisphere, that is to say; in the southern hemisphere, from late autumn to early spring). Globular clusters are remarkably regular, and may contain up to a million stars.

Also in the Galaxy we find clouds of gas and dust known as nebulae. A few of them are visible with the naked eye, and telescopes show vast numbers. Nebulae are stellar birthplaces, where fresh stars are being formed from the tenuous interstellar material. Around five thousand million years ago, our Sun was born inside a nebula in just this way.

Our Galaxy is by no means the only one. Modern equipment can reveal at least a thousand million others, but all are a long way away. Only a few are within a million light-years of us, and most are at immense distances. In the northern sky, the most famous outer galaxy is the Great Spiral in the constellation of Andromeda, which is dimly visible with the naked eye but very easy to see with binoculars. It is 2,200,000 light-years away, and is larger than our Galaxy, with more than our quota of 100 thousand million stars. Telescopes show that it is spiral in form, like a cosmic Catherine-wheel, and this is no surprise; there are many spiral galaxies, including our own. If we could see our Galaxy from 'above' or 'below', the spiral shape would be very evident. The Sun lies close to the edge of one of the spiral arms.

Even the Andromeda system is a relatively near neighbour, and most galaxies are so remote that they appear comparatively faint. Today we know of galaxies which are well over 10,000 million light-years away, so that we see them as they used to be when the universe was young. We also know that all the galaxies except those of our own particular 'local' group are racing away from us – and the further away they are, the faster they are going. This does not mean that we are particularly unpopular, or that we are in any privileged position. The entire universe is expanding, and every group of galaxies is receding from every other group.

How big is the universe, and how was it born? These are the most fundamental of all questions. I will discuss them later in this book, but I cannot hope to provide satisfactory answers. All we can really say is that the universe in its present form cannot be more than 20,000 million years old, and is probably rather younger; we may be able to set a limit to the size of the universe which we can see, but this is certainly not the whole story.

I hope that this 'roll-call' is of help, and at the end of the book I have added a glossary which may be useful. But there is one other point which is worth making here. On countless occasions during the past forty years or so people have said to me: 'What has happened to the stars? They used to be so much brighter than they are now; have they faded?' The answer, of course, is that they have not – but our skies have become brighter. Glaring artificial illuminations cast a sheen over the entire heavens, and light pollution has become a very serious problem, not only to astronomers. Sadly, anyone who lives inside a city or a densely-populated area will have at best a very poor view, and will certainly never be able to see the beauty of the Milky Way.

Efforts are being made to tackle the problem. It is not true to say, as some people have done, that astronomers want to 'put out the lights'; in the modern world, with the general breakdown in law and order, well-lit streets are essential. The aim is to provide lights which shine down, not up, and encouraging progress is being made; but there is a long way to go, and it would indeed be tragic if future generations were deprived of the glory of the night sky.

# 2

# THE
—— SPINNING SKY ——

It is easy to imagine that we are living on a steady, motionless Earth, but this is certainly not true. The Earth is turning on its axis once in 24 hours, so that we are being whirled about; the Earth is moving round the Sun at an average speed of around 66,000 m.p.h., and the Sun itself is travelling round the centre of the Galaxy at over 130 miles per second, taking us with it.

Our path round the Sun is not perfectly circular; like the orbits of all the other planets it is slightly elliptical, and our distance ranges between 91,400,000 miles in December out to 94,600,000 miles in June. The seasons have very little to do with the changing distance. The Earth's axis of rotation is tilted to the perpendicular to the orbit by 23½ degrees, and in December the north pole is tipped away from the Sun, so that it is winter in the northern hemisphere; in June it is the south pole which is tipped away, and the northern part of the world enjoys its summer.

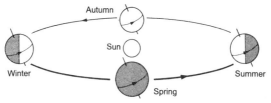

The seasons

Ancient peoples believed the Earth to be surrounded by a solid invisible crystal sphere, whose centre was coincident with the centre of the

Earth's globe. In some ways it is still very convenient to visualise this 'celestial sphere', and to assume that it really does revolve round the Earth in a period of 24 hours, carrying the Sun, Moon, planets and stars with it. We can then fix the positions of the celestial objects on the sphere, much the way in which we fix positions on the Earth by means of latitude and longitude.

The first step is to define the poles of the sky. These lie in the direction of the Earth's axis of rotation, as shown in the diagram. The north celestial pole is marked within one degree by the brightish star Polaris, in the constellation of Ursa Minor, the Little Bear; the opposite pole is not so favoured, and the south pole star, Sigma Octantis, is none too easy to see with the naked eye – something which southern navigators never cease to regret.

The celestial poles

It is easy to see that as the Earth spins, the Pole Star seems to remain motionless in the sky (or virtually so), with everything else turning round it. This is not to say that Polaris is important in itself; it owes its eminence to the fact that it chances to lie in the direction of the Earth's axis. This has not always been so, because of an effect known as precession. The Earth is not a perfect sphere; its diameter is 7926 miles as measured through the equator, but only 7900 miles as measured through the poles. The Sun and Moon pull on this equatorial bulge, and the result is that the Earth's axis wobbles slightly in the manner of a gyroscope which is running down. A gyroscope will wobble or 'precess' in a few seconds; the Earth's axis takes 25,800 years to complete a full turn, but it means that the position of the celestial pole changes slowly but steadily. At the time when the

Egyptian Pyramids were being built, the pole lay near a much fainter star, Thuban in Draco (the Dragon); it is now near Polaris, but it will not stay there, and in 12,000 years from now the north pole star will be Vega in Lyra (the Lyre), one of the most brilliant stars in the sky.

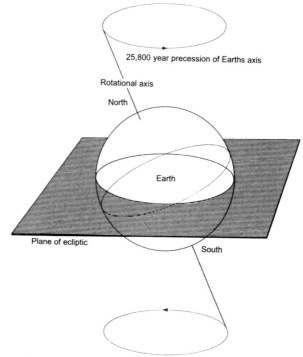

25,800 year precession of Earths axis

Rotational axis

North

Earth

Plane of ecliptic

South

Precession diagram

The altitude of the celestial pole above the horizon depends on the latitude of the observer on the Earth's surface. For example, if you find that Polaris is 60 degrees in altitude, you will know that your latitude is 60 degrees north, about the same as that of St. Petersburg. (For the moment, I propose to simplify matters by assuming that Polaris lies exactly at the polar point.) On the equator, Polaris will lie on the horizon – altitude 0 degrees – and from southern latitudes it can never be seen at all; we have to make do with the obscure Sigma Octantis.

If a star is sufficiently close to the pole, it will be circumpolar; that is to say, it will remain above the horizon all the time. For example,

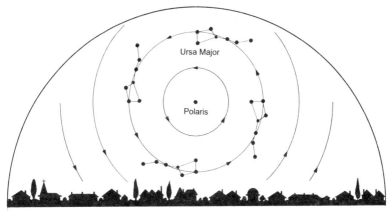

Circumpolar star diagram

consider Ursa Major, the Great Bear. It is in the far north of the sky, and from Britain it never sets; it merely goes round and round the pole, as shown in the previous diagram, whereas Regulus in Leo (the Lion), further away from the pole, spends part of its 24-hour circuit below the horizon. Go to a more southerly latitude, and you will find that the Bear is no longer circumpolar, though to compensate for this it becomes possible to see stars which are too far south in the sky to rise over Britain.

Just as the Earth's equator cuts the world in two, so the celestial equator cuts the sky in two; it is simply the projection of the Earth's equator on to the celestial sphere. On Earth, latitude is defined as the observer's angular distance north or south of the equator, as measured from the centre of the globe; approximately 51 degrees north for London, 38 degrees north for Athens, 12 degrees south for Darwin in Australia, 34 degrees south for Cape Town, and so on. Obviously, the latitude of the north pole is 90 degrees north, and that of the south pole 90 degrees south. To fix your position you need to know your longitude as well as your latitude, and here we measure the angle from the great circle on the Earth's globe which passes through both poles and also Greenwich Observatory in Outer London, as shown in the diagram. Greenwich was accepted as the zero for longitude during the 1880s, when international agreement was much easier to obtain than it is now.

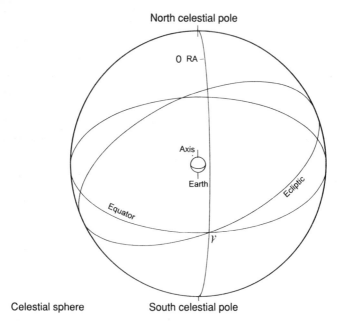

North celestial pole

Celestial sphere — South celestial pole

Now let us go back to the celestial sphere, and define the equivalents of latitude and longitude. Declination is simply the angular distance of the star (or other body) north or south of the celestial equator – for example 39 degrees north or +39° for Vega and 53 degrees south, or –53°, for Canopus in the constellation of Carina, the Keel. (Again I am using round numbers; the actual value for Vega is +38°47′01″.) This is the celestial equivalent of latitude, and presents no problems at all, but the equivalent of terrestrial longitude is rather less straightforward.

The apparent yearly path of the Sun round the sky is called the ecliptic; it may be defined as the projection of the Earth's orbit on to the celestial sphere. Since the axis is tilted to the perpendicular by 23½ degrees (more precisely 23°.44), this is also the angle between the ecliptic and the celestial equator. Therefore, the Sun's declination can range between 23½ degrees north and 23½ degrees south; the points of greatest declination are known as the solstices. The actual dates vary slightly because of the vagaries of our calendar, but not by more than a day or so; in 1994 the summer solstice fell on 21 June and the winter solstice on 22 December.

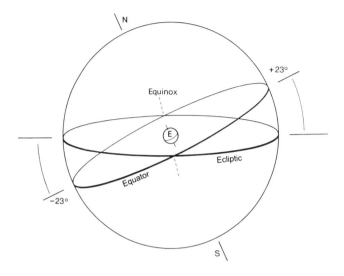

Ecliptic and equator

During its annual journey against the stars the Sun must cross the equator twice, once when travelling from south to north, around 20 March, and once when travelling from north to south, around 23 September. These two points are known as the equinoxes. They are not marked by any bright stars, and of course precession means that they shift slowly and inexorably, because a change in the position of the celestial pole also means a change in the position of the celestial equator. In Pyramid times the March or vernal equinox lay in the constellation of Aries, the Ram, and it is still known as the First Point of Aries, even though precession has long since moved it into the adjacent constellation of Pisces, the Fishes. It is the First Point of Aries which we take as the zero for the celestial equivalent of longitude, known as right ascension.

Right ascension is defined as the angular distance between the object and the First Point of Aries, but, rather confusingly, it is always given in units of time. As the Earth spins, a celestial body will rise in an easterly direction and set toward the west (unless it is circumpolar, when it will remain in view all the time). When it reaches its highest point above the horizon, it is said to culminate. The First Point of Aries must culminate once in every 24 hours, though naturally this often happens during daylight. The right ascension (R.A.) of a celestial body is given by the time-lapse between the culmination of the First Point of Aries and the culmination of the body. Thus Altair, a bright star in Aquila (the Eagle) culminates 19 hours 51 minutes after the First Point has done so; therefore, the R.A. of Altair is 19h 51m. Because the stars remain in virtually the same positions on the celestial sphere, their right ascensions and declinations do not alter except by a very slight annual shift due to precession, but the co-ordinates of the Sun, Moon and planets are changing all the time.

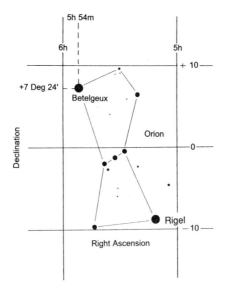

Right ascension

Given the declination of a star, you can easily work out whether it can be seen from your observing site. All that you have to do is to work out your co-latitude, which is simply your actual latitude subtracted from 90 degrees. My own home, at Selsey in Sussex, lies at latitude 51 degrees N, so that my co-latitude is $90 - 51 = 39°$. This means that any star north of declination +39° will never set, and any star south of declination –39° will never rise. I can always see Deneb in Cygnus, the

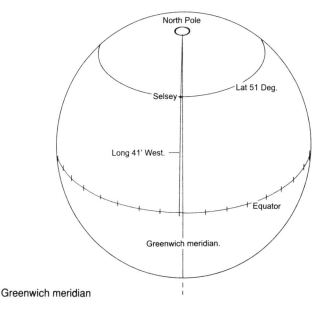

North Pole

Lat 51 Deg.

Selsey

Long 41' West.

Equator

Greenwich meridian.

Greenwich meridian

Swan (declination +45°), but I have no sight of Canopus (declination −53°). Invercargill, in New Zealand, lies at latitude 46 degrees south, so that from here Canopus is circumpolar and Deneb can never be seen.

When the Sun is north of the celestial equator, it is circumpolar from the north pole of the Earth, and this is why there is a six-months' 'day' there. When the Sun moves south of the equator it is the turn of the south pole to have its 'midnight sun', and at the moment plans are well advanced for setting up a major observatory right on the south pole itself. The site is expected to be particularly favourable astronomically; it will disturb nothing – even penguins avoid Central Antarctica! – and there are high hopes for the new observatory, though it must be admitted that conditions there will be somewhat chilly.

Certainly the celestial sphere is a useful concept, and at least it allows us to clarify the way in which we fix the positions of the objects in the sky – even though we no longer believe, as our forebears did, that the world is surrounded by a solid sphere.

# 3

# — SKY-WATCHERS —

A famous American was wrong when he once said that 'History is bunk'. It is not; and I doubt whether anyone can really appreciate a subject without knowing at least a little about its background. The story of astronomy goes back to our cave-dwelling ancestors, and to summarise it in a single chapter is a truly Himalayan task, but at least I can say a little about some of the main highlights.

Originally it was assumed that the Earth must be both flat and motionless. This was natural enough – after all, the Earth does look flat apart from local irregularities such as hills and valleys, and we have no sensation of being whirled along at breakneck speed. It was also assumed that the Sun, Moon and stars had been created for the specific benefit of Mankind, and, as we have noted, the sky was thought to be solid. (According to the Egyptians it was in fact the body of a goddess with the rather appropriate name of Nut, who was crouched over the flat earth in a decidedly inelegant position.) The sky revolved round the Earth once in 24 hours, carrying all the celestial bodies with it.

It is only with the development of writing that we have any positive information to guide us, but it seems that the constellation patterns date back to 3000 BC or even earlier. We cannot be sure, and neither do we know which peoples made the first attempt at sky-mapping; it may have been the Egyptians, the Chinese or even the Cretans. Certainly there were various different systems.

Naturally, the main emphasis was on observation, and in particular the Chinese records are most informative. There were good descriptions of unusual phenomena such as eclipses and comets, and the dates are given accurately, though of course the Chinese had no idea of the causes of these events. We know that an eclipse of the Sun is due to the temporary covering-up of the brilliant disk by the dark, invisible body of the Moon; the Chinese preferred to think that the Sun was being attacked by a hungry dragon, so that the only remedy was to scare the beast away by making as much noise as possible. (It always worked! Sadly, the old story that two Court astronomers named Hi and Ho were executed for failing to predict an eclipse has been discounted by modern scholars.) The first Chinese record of a solar eclipse goes back to 2136 BC. Comets were also studied, and were regarded with alarm, because it was thought they indicated divine displeasure – a feeling which is not quite dead even yet.

The Egyptians were avid sky-watchers, and there is no doubt that the Pyramids are astronomically aligned, but true astronomy began with the Greeks. It is often said that the 'Greek miracle' was rapid; actually it was nothing of the kind. Thales of Miletus, the first of the great philosophers, was born around 624 BC; Ptolemy of Alexandria, the last, died about AD 180 – giving a total span of over eight centuries, so that in time Ptolemy was as remote from Thales as we are from the Crusades. Yet it is true that the Greeks made amazing progress, and we can only admire them.

There were two great steps to be taken. One was to prove that the Earth is not flat, and the other was to show that it is moving round the Sun, so that it is not genuinely important and merely ranks as a normal planet. The first of these steps was taken at an early stage in the Greek story, and Aristotle, around 350 BC, knew quite well that the Earth is a globe. He was even able to give observational proof. First, he knew that the brilliant southern star Canopus can be seen from Alexandria, but not from the more northerly Athens; this is easy to explain if the world is spherical, but not if it is flat. Secondly, he knew that an eclipse of the Moon is caused by the shadow of the Earth falling on the lunar surface; since this shadow is curved, it follows that the Earth's surface must also be curved. Around 240 BC another philosopher, Eratosthenes of Cyrene, even made a remarkably accurate estimate of the Earth's size.

Later Greeks proved to be expert observers. Hipparchus of Nicaea, around 140 BC (all our BC dates are bound to be somewhat uncertain) drew up a good star catalogue, and the accuracy of his measurements is shown by the fact that he discovered the pheno-menon of precession. Between AD 140 and 180 Ptolemy of Alexandria extended and improved Hipparchus' catalogue, and also produced the first map of the world which was based upon astronomical observa-tion rather than guesswork. It was reasonably good, though naturally it covered only the Mediterranean and adjacent areas (Britain is shown, though Scotland is joined on to England at a curious angle). It was Ptolemy, too, who wrote a great book which has come down to us by way of its Arab translation, and is usually called the *Almagest*. It is really a compendium of ancient science, and its value to historians has been incalculable.

What the Greeks could not bring themselves to do was to dethrone the Earth from its proud central position. A few of the philosophers, notably Aristarchus of Samos around 280 BC, did take this drastic step, but as they could give no proof they found few followers, and the later philosophers went back to the idea of an all-important central Earth. This is always termed the Ptolemaic system, even though Ptolemy himself did not invent it, and only brought it to its highest degree of perfection.

According to Ptolemy, the Earth lay in the centre of the universe, with the Moon, Sun, and planets and stars moving round it; the stars were carried on the outer crystal sphere, and other spheres carried the members of the Solar System. All orbits had to be circular, because the circle is the 'perfect' form, and nothing short of absolute perfection can be allowed in the heavens. The trouble about this idea was that the movements of the planets were not regular, and so could not be explained by uniform circular motion. Ptolemy, who was an excellent mathematician, knew this quite well, and was forced to adopt a cumbersome system with each planet moving round the Earth in a small circle or epicycle, the centre of which – the deferent – itself moved round the Earth in a perfect circle. In the end the whole plan became hopelessly involved and unwieldy, but it did fit the observations, and not for many centuries was it seriously challenged.

After Ptolemy's death the Dark Ages descended over Europe, and there was a period of stagnation, though there was an important development around AD 570 when Isidorus, Bishop of Seville, became the first major figure to draw a clear distinction between astronomy and astrology. The revival of astronomy was due to the Arabs, from the early 9th century; they drew up accurate star catalogues, and

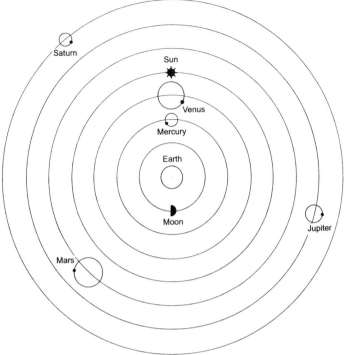

Ptolemaic system

measured the movements of the Sun, Moon and planets more precise-ly than Ptolemy had been able to do, though admittedly their main aim was astrological. In 1433 Ulugh Beigh, one of the most powerful of the Oriental rulers, set up an elaborate observatory at his capital at Samarkand, and new, improved planetary tables were produced. But with Ulugh Beigh's murder the Arab school came to an end, and subsequent developments were chiefly European.

The next important step was taken in the sixteenth century by a Polish churchman whose name was Mikołaj Kopernik, but who is always known to us as Copernicus. He had made careful studies of the movements of the planets, and realised that the Ptolemaic theory was hopelessly artificial; most of the difficulties could be removed by the simple expedient of taking the Earth away from the centre of the system and putting the Sun there instead. He was well aware that the Church would accuse him of heresy, and he withheld publication until the very end of his life, in 1543. This was a wise precaution, and the Church leaders lost no time in launching fierce attacks on him. Martin Luther referred to him as 'this fool who wants to turn the heavens upside-down', and persecution began; in 1600 one Copernican supporter, Giordano Bruno, was actually burned at the stake in Rome partly because of his expressed belief that the Earth moves round the Sun.

Adopting the Sun-centred or 'heliocentric' theory was Copernicus' only major achievement; most of his other conclusions were wrong, and he was wedded to the concept of perfectly circular orbits, so that he was even reduced to bringing back Ptolemy's epicycles. Yet he had taken the essential step, and his book, *De Revolutionibus Orbium Coelestium*, marked the beginning of the greatest of all revolutions in astronomical thought.

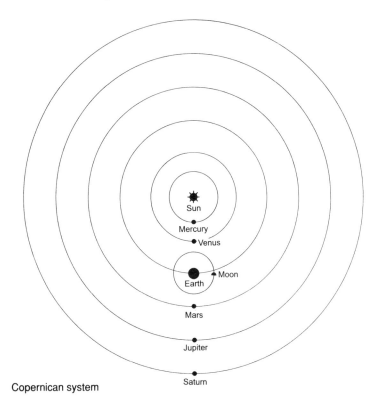

Copernican system

Ironically, the next main character in the story, the Danish nobleman Tycho Brahe, was no Copernican; he could not believe that the Earth could be relegated to the status of a mere planet, and he worked out a weird hybrid system of his own which satisfied nobody. However, he was a superbly accurate observer, and between 1576 and 1596 he worked away at his observatory at Hven, an island in the Baltic, compiling a star catalogue which was incomparably better than any of its predecessors. He also made careful measurements of the movements of the planets, particularly Mars. When he died, in 1601, his work fell into the hands of his last assistant, a young German mathematician named Johannes Kepler, and the stage was set for the next major advance.

Tycho and Kepler were very different from each other. Tycho was haughty and ruthless, with a wonderful sense of his own importance (during his student days he lost part of his nose in a duel, and made himself a new one out of gold, silver and wax). Kepler was a frail, neurotic man, some of whose theories seem to belong to the mediaeval period rather than to the more modern age. But Kepler had implicit faith in Tycho's observations, and after years of work he found the answer to the main problem. The planets do indeed move round the Sun, but they do so in orbits which are elliptical rather than circular. Finally Kepler was able to draw up his three Laws of Planetary Motion, upon which all later work has been based. The first two Laws were published in 1609, and the third in 1618.

Time taken to move from AB to AC is the same as the time taken to travel from AD to AC. The area ABF is equal to the area FCD.

Kepler's Laws

The first Law states that a planet moves in an elliptical path; the Sun occupies one focus of the ellipse, while the other focus is empty. Law 2 states that the radius vector (i.e. an imaginary line joining the centre of the planet to the centre of the Sun) sweeps out equal areas in equal times; in other words, a planet moves fastest when it is at its closest to the Sun (perihelion) and slowest when it is furthest out (aphelion). The third Law gives a link between a planet's orbital period and its distance from the Sun, so that it becomes possible to draw up a complete scale model of the Solar System.

It is worth noting here that most planetary orbits are not very different from circles; draw the Earth's path on a scale fitting this page, and it would be almost indistinguishable from a circle. Mars, upon which Kepler concentrated, has a rather more eccentric path, and the difference between its perihelion and aphelion is over twenty million miles; however, Kepler's work was a brilliant piece of mathematical investigation. Meanwhile, telescopes had been invented.

It is widely believed that the first telescopes were made in Holland, in 1608. It is true that these are the first telescopes of whose existence we have conclusive proof, but research by the British historian C. A. Ronan now seems to have established that a curious kind of telescope was made by Leonard Digges, in England, at some time between 1550 and 1560, in which case he preceded the Dutch by over half a century. The Digges telescope appears to have used both mirrors and lenses; whether it was ever turned skyward we do not know, and neither have we an accurate idea of what it looked like. So astronomically, at least, telescopes come into the picture at around the time that Kepler was publishing his first Laws. Thomas Harriot, one-time tutor to Sir Walter Raleigh, drew a telescopic map of the Moon in 1609, but the first systematic observer was Galileo Galilei, the great Italian scientist who was also the true founder of experimental mechanics.

Galileo heard of the Dutch invention, copied and improved it, and used it to make a series of spectacular discoveries, confirming that Copernicus had been right in believing that the Earth moves round the Sun. Galileo saw the mountains and craters of the Moon; the countless stars of the Milky Way; the four bright satellites of Jupiter, proving at least that the Earth is not the only centre of motion in the universe; and, even more significantly, the phases of Venus. Because Venus is closer to the Sun than we are, it shows phases similar to those of the Moon, and for much the same reason. The point is that in Ptolemy's theory, Venus could never show a complete cycle of phases from new to full.

Unlike Kepler, Galileo was not cautious. He not only published his beliefs, but did so in a way which was tactless enough to offend the Holy See. He was accused of heresy, brought to trial by the Inquisition, and forced into a hollow and completely meaningless recantation. His major work, the *Dialogues*, remained on the Papal Index of forbidden books until 1836, and it was not until 1993 that the Vatican finally admitted that Galileo had been right all along!

The Ptolemaic theory was eventually abandoned in 1687, with the publication of Isaac Newton's immortal *Principia*, in which Newton laid down the laws of gravitation and ushered in the modern scientific era. This book has been described as the greatest mental effort ever made by one man, but it was by no means Newton's only achievement. It was he who used a glass prism to split up sunlight and show that it is made up of a combination of all colours of the rainbow, thereby introducing the science of spectroscopy; and in 1671 he presented the Royal Society with a telescope of entirely new type.

Galileo's telescope was a refractor, collecting its light by means of a glass lens. One problem was that the lens produced false colour, so that an object such as a star was surrounded by gaudy rings which may have looked beautiful, but were most certainly unwanted. The initial remedy was to build telescopes of immense length, making them awkward to use; in extreme cases, the main lens had to be fixed to the top of a mast. Newton decided to do away with the object-glass altogether, and to collect the light by using a curved mirror, which reflects all the colours equally. Newton's first 'reflector' had a main mirror one inch across; today the world's largest telescope has a mirror almost 400 inches in diameter. We have come a long way in little over three centuries.

It was around this time that the first telescopically equipped observatories were established. So far as Britain was concerned, the main need was navigational, because there had been several naval disasters due to the fact that the commanders simply did not know where they were after spending weeks or months out at sea. Latitude-finding was easy enough; all that had to be done was to measure the altitude of the Pole Star, and then make a minor correction to allow for the fact that the Pole Star is not exactly at the pole. It was longitude-finding which was the main problem. Once the exact 'ship's time' was known and compared with the time at Greenwich, longitude could be worked out; but there were no clocks accurate enough to function properly at sea. The alternative was to use the changing position of the Moon as a sort of natural clock-hand, and measure its movements against the stars. This involved having a very accurate star catalogue, and even Tycho Brahe's was not good enough, because it had been compiled solely on the basis of naked-eye observations. (It is ironical that Tycho died just before the telescope became readily available; he would have made such good use of it!) Accordingly, that much-maligned monarch King Charles II ordered that a new observatory should be built and equipped with a telescope, so that the astronomer in charge could set to work in compiling a catalogue good enough to satisfy the sailors. The chosen site was Greenwich Park, in Outer London, and the Rev. John Flamsteed was appointed Astronomer Royal. He did eventually produce the required catalogue, though it took him a long time, and by the time it was finished the whole method of 'lunar distances' had become obsolete because of the development of accurate marine chronometers.

Flamsteed was succeeded by Edmond Halley, best remembered now because of his association with the comet which bears his name. Since then, the Royal Greenwich Observatory has remained in the forefront of research, though it is no longer in London. The original building – designed, incidentally, by Sir Christopher Wren – has been turned into a museum.

Next we come to the career of William Herschel, a Hanoverian musician who came to England while still a young man, and spent the rest of his life there. For a while he was organist at the fashionable resort of Bath Spa, but his main interest was astronomical, and he built his own reflecting telescopes. With one of these, in 1781, he discovered a new planet, now known to us as Uranus. The discovery made Herschel famous; a grant from King George III of England and Hanover made it possible for him to abandon music as a profession, and he devoted himself to 'reviews of the heavens', his main aim being to find out the way in which the stars are arranged in space. By then it was known that the stars are suns, and that they are very remote indeed; Herschel failed to measure their distances, but during his work he made countless important discoveries, so that he is often regarded as the greatest observer of all time. He came to the conclusion that the Galaxy must be a flattened system, and in this he was of course correct, though he erred in placing the Sun near the middle of the system. His largest telescope was a reflector with a 49-inch mirror and a focal length of 40 feet, though most of his best work was carried out with smaller and more manageable instruments. Other observers were active at the same time – for example Charles Messier, who compiled the famous catalogue of star-clusters and nebulae, and Johann Hieronymus Schröter, who concentrated upon observations of the Moon and planets.

Up to the end of the eighteenth century almost all astronomers had been based in the Earth's northern hemisphere, so that the stars of the far south had been neglected. During the 1830s Sir John Herschel, son of William, took a telescope to the Cape of Good Hope and made the first detailed survey of the southern sky, adding to his father's amazingly numerous discoveries of objects such as double stars, clusters and nebulae. It was at this time, too, that photography began to play a significant role, and as the years passed by the camera began to supersede the human eye for most branches of observation. The change-over was virtually complete well before the end of the century.

One fascinating development came from Ireland. At Birr Castle, in the middle of the island, the third Earl of Rosse built a monster telescope with a 72-inch mirror, much the largest ever made up to that time. It was clumsy and unwieldy, but it worked well, and Lord Rosse used it to great effect. He found that some of the nebulae seen by Herschel, Messier and others looked as though they were made of shining gas, but others were starry, and many of these were spiral in shape. Was it possible that these 'spiral nebulae' were external galaxies, rather than being mere minor features of the Milky Way? It was difficult to tell. In 1838 the German astronomer Friedrich Bessel had managed to make the first measurement of the distance of a star, and had shown that 61 Cygni, a dim star in the constellation of the Swan, lay at a distance of around 11 light-years, corresponding to 60 million million miles; but the spirals were clearly far more remote than this, and the problem of their status was not solved until 1923, but at least Herschel, Rosse and others had made the suggestion.

In 1666 Newton had broken sunlight into its constituent colours. It was not until a century and a half later that the German optician

Josef Fraunhofer made the first close study of the nature of sunlight, and a full explanation had to wait until 1858, when two of Fraunhofer's countrymen, Kirchhoff and Bunsen, showed that by using spectroscopes it was possible to find out 'what the stars are made of'. Today the spectroscope may be said to be the main research tool of the astronomer, and without it our knowledge of the universe would indeed be meagre.

Mathematical astronomy, too, had made great strides. In 1846 the new planet Neptune was tracked down because of the pull it had exerted upon Uranus, and this gave a final vindication of Newton's theories.

The Rosse 72-inch reflector was soon overtaken. Very powerful refractors were built; the largest of all, at the Yerkes Observatory in the United States, was given a 40-inch lens. It was completed in 1897, and is not likely to be surpassed, because there is a limit to the size of a useful lens; if too large and heavy it will distort under its own weight, ruining its performance – remember that a lens has to be supported all round its edge. Reflectors took over, with mirrors made up of glass rather than metal as in the Rosse telescope. The lead was taken by George Ellery Hale, an American who not only planned large telescopes but also persuaded friendly millionaires to finance them. Hale set up a 60-inch reflector on Mount Wilson in California, and followed this in 1917 with a 100-inch, which remained in a class of its own for more than three decades. It was with this telescope that Edwin Hubble was able to make the observations proving that the 'spiral nebulae' were, after all, independent galaxies far beyond our own. It was also Hubble who first demonstrated that the galaxies are racing away from us, and that the whole universe is expanding.

Mount Wilson is a lofty peak. Hale knew that the atmosphere is the main enemy of the astronomer; it is dirty and unsteady, and moreover it blocks out many of the important radiations coming from space. The solution is to 'go up' and this is why most great modern observatories are situated at high altitude – 14,000 feet in the case of the observatory on the summit of Mauna Kea, in Hawaii. There is also a tendency to concentrate upon the southern hemisphere, both because conditions there are generally better than those in the north and also because many of the most interesting objects in the sky are so far south that they never rise over Europe or mainland United States.

The major telescopes of today bear little resemblance to those of the past – even the relatively recent past. The Mount Wilson 100-inch is no longer among the world's largest; the palm now goes to the Keck telescope on Mauna Kea, which has a segmented mirror with a total diameter of no less than 387 inches. Even larger instruments are in advanced stages of planning, and will enable us to peer out into the far reaches of the universe.

Until our own century, astronomers were limited to studying the rays of visible light coming to us from space, but in 1931 came the birth of radio astronomy. Light is a wave-motion, and the colour of the light depends upon its wavelength – that is to say, the distance between successive wave-crests. Red light has the longest wavelength and violet the shortest, though even for red light the wavelength is tiny by normal standards – about 7500 Ångströms (one Ångström being equal to one hundred-millionth part of a centimetre; the name honours the last-century Swedish physicist Anders Ångström). But visible light is only a small part of the total range of wavelengths, or electromagnetic spectrum. To the long-wave end of red we have infra-red, microwaves and then radio waves; to the short-wave end we have ultra-violet,

Electromagnetic spectrum

X-rays and the very short gamma-rays. Very few of these 'invisible radiations' can reach ground level, because they are blocked out by layers in the Earth's upper air, but some can, and in particular there is a 'window' in the radio range. In 1931 Karl Jansky, a Czech-born American radio engineer, was carrying out investigations into static, using an improvised aerial, when he found that he was picking up radio emissions from the Milky Way. Curiously, he never followed up this discovery as he might have been expected to do, but after the end of the war radio astronomy became a vitally important branch of science; Sir Bernard Lovell master-minded the huge 250-foot radio 'dish' telescope at Jodrell Bank, in Cheshire, which came into operation in 1957, and by now there are many radio arrays all over the world. Of course, a radio telescope does not produce a visible picture in the same way as an optical telescope, and one certainly cannot look through it. It is more in the nature of a large aerial, but it can provide information which we could never obtain in any other way.

The Space Age began on 4 October 1957, with a very pronounced bang. The Russians launched the first of all artificial satellites, Sputnik 1, which was football-sized and carried little apart from a radio transmitter, but which ushered in a new era. It soon became possible to send sophisticated equipment above the atmosphere, and to study the radiations which can never reach ground level; for example X-ray astronomy began in 1962, when a rocket-borne detector tracked down the first discrete celestial X-ray source. The first probes to the Moon were dispatched in 1959; manned flight began two years later, with the epic journey of Yuri Gagarin, and before long manned journeys were common, culminating in the pioneer Moon landing by Neil Armstrong and Buzz Aldrin in July 1969. Meanwhile, automatic probes were being sent to the planets, and by now all the principal members of the Sun's family have been surveyed from close range (unless we include Pluto). There have even been controlled landings on Mars and Venus. It is probably true to say that we have learned more about the planets during the last forty years than we had been able to do for the previous forty centuries.

Optical telescopes have been improved beyond all recognition; the Keck reflector atop Mauna Kea has been joined by a twin instrument, and when working together the two could, in theory, distinguish a car's headlights separately from a range of 16,000 miles. But all ground-based telescopes are handicapped by having to look through the atmosphere, and this is why a space telescope was planned. It was launched in 1990, and put into an orbit round the Earth over 350 miles above ground level; it has a 94-inch mirror, and 'seeing' conditions are perfect all the time, so that it can out-perform any telescope operating from the Earth's surface. Fittingly, it was named in honour of Edwin Hubble.

Just as photography superseded visual observation a century ago, so photography itself is now being superseded by electronic equipment. CCDs – Charge-Coupled Devices – are far more sensitive than any photographic plate, and have largely taken over, which means that telescopes built years ago are now much more powerful than they originally were. No longer does an astronomer have to spend long hours in a cold, darkened dome, checking on his photographic exposures. Today, he sits in the comfort of a control room, watching a television screen. He need not be in the dome at all, or even in the same country. It is quite practicable for an astronomer in, say, Edinburgh to control a telescope in Hawaii.

I realise that this has been a very breathless and sketchy account of events over the ages, but I hope that it will help in setting the scene. Modern astronomy is a dynamic science; every year brings its quota of new discoveries and new surprises. We have learned a great deal, though we cannot yet pretend to have more than a vague understanding of the great universe in which we all live.

# 4

# THE
# — ASTRONOMER'S —
# TELESCOPE

If you become seriously interested in astronomy, then sooner or later you will want to equip yourself with a telescope. This is often where the trouble begins, because a telescope is either good or cheap – not both. It is unwise to spend much money on a refracting telescope with a main lens less than 3 inches across, or a Newtonian reflector with a mirror smaller than 6 inches. These telescopes are simply too small to be at all satisfactory, and it is far better to invest in a pair of good binoculars, which have most of the advantages of a small telescope apart from sheer magnification, and which can be bought at comparatively low cost. They can also be used for everyday viewing, such as bird-watching, whereas a conventional astronomical telescope cannot, partly because of the small field of view and partly because it gives an upside-down image.

Binoculars are classified according to their magnification and the diameter of the main object-glass, always given in millimetres. Thus a 7 x 50 pair gives a power of 7, with each object-glass 50 mm across. This is very suitable, because a higher magnification – at least above x 12 – means that the binoculars become so unwieldy that they are difficult to hand-hold. (Remember not to look anywhere near the Sun. I will have more to say about this later, but I do not apologise for stressing it, because it is so important.)

The principle of the refractor is shown in the diagram. Light from the object under study passes through the object-glass, and the rays are bunched up and brought to focus, where the image is magnified by a second lens known as an eyepiece or ocular. Note that it is the object-

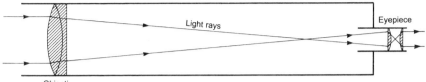

Objective

Refractor principle

glass which is responsible for the light-collection, while all the actual magnification is carried out by the eyepiece – and if you see a telescope advertised as 'magnifying' so many times, without any mention of the size of the object-glass, avoid it completely. The distance between the object-glass and the focus is termed the focal length. Generally you will need at least three eyepieces, one giving low power for general views, one giving medium power for more detailed work, and one yielding high power for use on the Moon or planets under really good conditions.

Newtonian reflector

The commonest form of reflecting telescope is the Newtonian (no prizes are offered for guessing who first worked out this system). The light passes down an open tube, which may be a skeleton, and falls upon a curved mirror at the far end. This parabolic speculum sends the light back up the tube, directing it on to a smaller, flat mirror inclined at an angle of 45 degrees. The flat sends the rays into the side of the tube, where they are brought to focus and the image is enlarged by an eyepiece as before. With a Newtonian, then, the observer looks into the side of the tube instead of up it, and it is almost essential to have a finder telescope attached to the main tube.

Each type has its own advantages – and, unfortunately, its own drawbacks. Inch for inch, the refractor is the more effective of the two; it is also sturdier, and if well treated will not need drastic maintenance for many years, while reflectors are much more temperamental, quite apart from the fact that their mirrors have to be periodically recoated with either aluminium or silver. Against this, a Newtonian reflector is much cheaper than a refractor of comparable performance, and it does not produce the irritating false colour which so plagued the early observers (though it must be added that modern compound object-glasses reduce this trouble to a bare minimum). There are many other optical systems; for example there is the Cassegrain, where the

Cassegrain reflector

secondary mirror is convex rather than flat, and the light is sent back to the eyepiece via a hole in the main speculum. There are 'folded' telescopes which use both mirrors and lenses, and these are very convenient, particularly as they are easy to move around; their main drawback is their cost.

Mountings are of two main types. An altazimuth stand means that the telescope can be moved freely in any direction, either in altitude (up or down) or azimuth (east or west). The problem here is that two motions have to be considered, and guiding is not easy when a high magnification is being used; it is amazing how quickly a celestial object will shoot across the field of view! Neither can an altazimuth telescope be used for photography, except in a very limited sense. This also applies to the increasingly-popular 'Dobsonian', which is elementary but, in its way, effective.

With an equatorial mounting, the telescope is set upon an axis pointing to the celestial pole, so that only one movement has to be taken into account – east to west. The up or down motion is automatic, and the addition of a mechanical drive means that the target object can be kept firmly in the field of view.

Until recently all major telescopes were equatorially mounted, but modern-type computers make it possible to drive an altazimuth with equal precision, and in many ways the altazimuth is far more convenient. For example, consider the 138-inch NTT or New Technology Telescope at La Silla in the Atacama Desert, the Chilean station of

Dobsonian

German Equatorial

Mountings for telescopes

the European Southern Observatory. Here the telescope itself can move only in altitude, and the entire observatory rotates with it, so that the slit is always in front of the instrument, and the observatory looks nothing like the graceful domes of yesteryear. Moreover, the mirror has its shape controlled by computer-driven 'pads', adjusting the shape whenever the mirror is turned around. This 'active optics' technique is now becoming common, and has been followed by the 'adaptive optics' system, which uses a second small mirror to allow for disturbances in the Earth's atmosphere.

Obviously there is a limit to the size of a single mirror. The Russians completed a 236-inch instrument as long ago as 1975, and it remains the largest operating single-mirror telescope in the world, though it will certainly be surpassed before the end of the twentieth century. The previous holder of the record was the 200-inch Hale reflector at

Palomar in California, dating back to 1948. Though the 200-inch has always been a great success (and is still in the forefront of research, particularly since it is now used with electronic devices such as CCDs) the Russian giant was not. The optics were inferior, and the site at Mount Pastukhov in the old USSR could not compare with that of other major observatories. Yet the 236-inch did make one vital contribution; it was the first really large telescope to be set upon a computer-controlled altazimuth mount.

The largest of all mirrors today is that of the Keck telescope atop Mauna Kea, in Hawaii. The diameter of the mirror is 387 inches (9.82 metres), but there was never any question of casting it from a single glass disk; it is made up of 36 segments, fitted together to form the correct optical curve. In 1996 a second Keck telescope – an identical twin – was set up close beside it; working together, the Kecks would be capable of detecting a car's head lights, separately, over a range of 16,000 miles. Other comparable projects are being planned, notably the VLT or Very Large Telescope, a combination of four 8-metre telescopes which, when working together, will have the light-grasp of a single 16-metre mirror. The VLT will be set up at Cerro Paranal, in Northern Chile, and should be working by the year 2000.

Most new observatories are being built at high altitude, well above the densest part of the Earth's atmosphere. Britain's largest telescope, appropriately named in honour of William Herschel, has been set up on the summit of the Roque de los Muchachos, an extinct volcano at La Palma in the Canary Islands, at over 8000 feet. Here too is the 100-inch Isaac Newton reflector, originally used at Herstmonceux in Sussex, the site of the transferred Royal Greenwich Observatory. La Palma (not Las Palmas, please note!) is a Spanish island, but the volcano-top is the home for telescopes from many nations, and certainly it is true that astronomy is an international science.

Various telescopes have been designed for special purposes. For example the UKIRT or United Kingdom Infra-Red Telescope, on Mauna Kea, has a thin mirror 150 inches across. It was intended solely for infra-red work, and this meant that the mirror could be of relatively low accuracy, though in the event it proved to be so good that it could be used for optical work as well. Solar telescopes catch their light by a rotatable coelostat, and the Sun's rays can then be sent down a tower or inclined plane to a laboratory where heavy fixed equipment is used for analysis.

In a way it is sad to see the eclipse of the large refracting telescope! Most of these are old, dating back to the nineteenth century, and few are now used for regular research, but they have played their part. At the Lowell Observatory at Flagstaff in Arizona the great 24-inch refractor is now used almost entirely for public viewing; it is a superb instrument, as I well know, because in the pre-Moon voyage days I used it extensively for mapping the lunar surface. The largest refractor in Britain, the 26-inch at Herstmonceux, was left idle for years following the departure of the Royal Greenwich Observatory, but at my suggestion it was brought back into operation recently, and it is still extremely useful. There is something peculiarly satisfying about a huge refractor, and it is ideal for visual studies of the Moon and planets.

Then, of course, there is the Hubble Space Telescope or HST, orbiting the world at a height of over 350 miles. It was launched in the Space Shuttle in 1990; it has a 94-inch mirror, and operates under perfect conditions of seeing. When it had been placed in orbit, it was found that the mirror had been wrongly figured, so that the performance was well below expectations. In 1993 a team of astronauts went up in a Shuttle, captured the telescope, installed corrective optics and returned it to orbit, so that it is now every bit as good as had originally been hoped. A second servicing mission was carried out in 1997.

A modern observatory such as those at Mauna Kea or La Palma is almost a city in itself, with instruments of all kinds as well as laboratories, offices and living quarters, but there are also many private observatories, and if you have a telescope of fair size it is desirable to have a permanent mount. A back-garden observatory may be a simple run-off shed, a building with a sliding or removable roof, or a proper dome; the cost is quite reasonable, and a run-off shed at least is very easy to make.

Note, too, that once you have acquired a good telescope, it will last you for a lifetime. And all things considered, the financial outlay is not exorbitant. An adequate telescope costs less than a couple of rail tickets between, say, London and Edinburgh, and it will give its owner endless enjoyment.

# 5
# INTO
# SPACE

The concept of space-travel is very old. Men have long dreamed of breaking free from the Earth, and in the second century AD a Greek satirist, Lucian of Samosata, went so far as to write a story about a flight to the Moon. He called it the *True History*, because, in his own words, it was made up of nothing but lies from beginning to end. He explained how a ship passing through the Pillars of Hercules, now known to us as the Straits of Gibraltar, was caught up in a water-spout, and hurled upward so violently that after seven days and seven nights it reached the Moon – where the sailors found that they had arrived at a fascinating time; the King of the Moon was about to do battle with the King of the Sun with regard to who should have first claim on Venus (the planet, I hasten to add, not the goddess). Later means of propulsion involved bird-power, fire-crackers and even demons. Finally, in 1865, the first scientific method was described. It did not work, and could never do so, but it was of value none the less.

The author was Jules Verne, the great French story-teller. In his novel *From the Earth to the Moon* three adventurers climb inside a projectile, and are fired Moonward at a speed of seven miles per second. Verne believed in being as accurate as possible, and he did give the correct speed for departure; but there were several things that he either did not know or else chose to ignore. First, starting off at seven miles per second would be quite a jerk, to put it mildly, and would at once reduce the luckless travellers to jelly. Secondly, air sets up resistance, and resistance causes heat; even before it left the barrel of the gun the projectile would have been burned away. And thirdly, the journey would be one-way only (though it is true that in his novel Verne cleverly avoided this particular difficulty).

Why seven miles per second? This is the Earth's escape velocity.
Throw an object upward, and it will rise to a certain height before
falling back. Throw it faster, and it will rise higher. At an initial
speed of seven miles per second (approximately 25,000 m.p.h.) it
would never return at all; the Earth's gravitational pull would not be

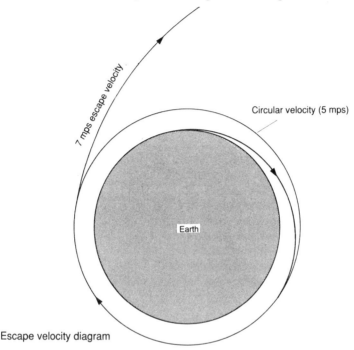

Escape velocity diagram

strong enough to draw it back, and the object would escape into space.
(The escape velocity of a body depends upon its mass; for example the
Moon has only 1/81 of the mass of the Earth, and the lunar escape
velocity is no more than one and a half miles per second.)

Space-guns being rejected, we come back to the only device which will
operate in airless space: the rocket. The principle is exactly the same
as with the firework rockets which Britons fire on 5 November each
year in memory of Guy Fawkes (who, some people claim, is the one
man we now need in Parliament). The firework consists of a hollow
tube filled with gunpowder, plus a stick to add stability. When the
touch-paper is lit, the gunpowder starts to burn; gas is shot out of the
exhaust, and 'kicks' the tube in the opposite direction. So long as the

Action     Reaction

Rocket principle

gas continues to stream out, the rocket will continue to fly. Atmosphere is not needed, and is actually a nuisance, because it sets up resistance and has to be pushed out of the way. We depend upon what Newton called the principle of reaction – 'every action has an equal and opposite reaction'.

There is a good way to demonstrate what is meant. Put a book on the floor, stand on the book and jump off. You will go one way, and the book will go in the opposite direction, because you have kicked against it; the effect would be the same if you were in airless space (assuming that you could survive there). So if we want to invade space, rockets must be our means of travel.

The first truly scientific suggestion was made a century ago by a shy, deaf Russian schoolteacher who rejoiced in the name of Konstantin Eduardovich Tsiolkovskii. He realised that solid fuels are inadequate, and so he proposed a proper rocket motor, in which two liquids – say petrol and liquid oxygen – are forced into a combustion chamber, where they react to produce the gas sent out from the exhaust. Tsiolkovskii also suggested mounting rockets one on top of the other, so that in effect the uppermost stage would be given a running start into space. At the time his work caused no interest whatsoever, partly because it was published in an obscure Russian journal; but by the time of his death, in 1934, he had become recognised as the 'father of space-flight', even though he was not a practical experimenter and never personally fired a rocket in his life.

The first liquid-fuel rocket was sent up in 1926 by an American, Robert Hutchings Goddard, who had never heard of Tsiolkovskii's work. His rocket was modest enough, rising to a height of a few tens of feet at a maximum speed of 60 m.p.h., but it showed that the principle was valid. A few years later a German team set up an experimental research station near Berlin, and began to build bigger and better rockets, but before long the politicians stepped in. The German government swooped on the rocketeers and transferred its leading members, including Wernher von Braun, to Peenemünde, an island in the Baltic, with orders to produce weapons for the coming war. It was here that von Braun and his colleagues produced the V2 weapons used to bombard England during 1944 and 1945. Of course they were purely military, but they were rockets none the less, and they were the direct ancestors of the space-ships of today. After the German collapse, the experimenters were transferred to America, and by 1949 the upper stage of a purely scientific rocket had soared to the dizzy height of almost 250 miles. There was great activity at Cape Canaveral in Florida, the main rocket base, and by 1955 the White House felt confident enough to state that an artificial satellite would be launched at some time during 1957 or 1958.

As we all remember, the Americans were forestalled. Russia's Sputnik 1 opened the Space Age on 4 October 1957; it entered a closed orbit round the Earth, sending back the never-to-be-forgotten 'Bleep! bleep!' signals. Other Russian satellites followed, and then, in 1958, Wernher von Braun master-minded the first American artificial satellite, Explorer 1. The 'race into space' was under way.

If an object is put into orbit with a velocity of five miles per second, it will not fall down, any more than the Moon does; it will continue circling the world indefinitely – unless any part of its orbit brings it down into the denser part of the atmosphere, so that it will be braked by friction and will eventually spiral to destruction (as happened to Sputnik 1 in early January 1958). Once the breakthrough had been achieved, satellites of all kinds were launched. Some carried scientific instruments to study radiations which are inaccessible from ground level (X-rays, for example); some were used for radio and television relays; others, regrettably, for military purposes.

Four years after Sputnik 1, the first man went into space. Predictably, he was a Russian – Yuri Gagarin – and he completed a full circuit of the Earth in his cramped capsule, Vostok 1, before landing safely in the prearranged part of what was then the Soviet Union. Up to that time it had been feared that space would be a hopelessly hostile environment. For example, there was potential danger from cosmic rays, which are not rays at all, but high-speed atomic particles bombarding the Earth from all directions all the time, though the 'heavy' particles are broken up in the high atmosphere and reduced to harmless fragments. Meteoroids were another cause of anxiety. But

Orbital speed. Diagram A shows ballistic trajectory, diagram B shows orbital trajectory

above all there was the question of weightlessness, or zero gravity. How would the human body react?

When in orbit round the Earth – in what is termed free fall – an astronaut has no apparent weight, not because he has 'got out of gravity' (which is theoretically impossible) but because he is neutralising it. To show what is meant, put a coin on top of a book and hold it out at arm's-length. The coin is pressing on the book, so that with reference to the book the coin is 'heavy'. Now drop the book. During the descent to the floor, the two are moving in the same direction at the same rate; the coin ceases to press on the book, so that with reference to the book it has become weightless (the effect would be just the same if the two were moving up, not down). Similarly, an orbiting astronaut will cease to press on his rocket, and will be weightless. Fortunately the effects have turned out not to be harmful, at least in the short term, and I remember Gagarin himself telling me that he found zero gravity 'very pleasant'! It was sad that Gagarin was killed in an ordinary aircraft crash a few years later.

Before long, two-man and even more elaborate vehicles were sent up, and women joined in (Valentina Tereshkova, in 1963, was the first). By the 1970s genuine space-stations had been launched, beginning with America's Skylab, which was manned by three successive crews and carried telescopes and scientific equipment of all kinds. By 1988 the ambitious Russian space-station Mir (still in orbit in 1996) had been 'home' for two cosmonauts for more than a year.

One obvious need was for a ferry-vehicle capable of taking crews and supplies up and down to space-stations. Using a new vehicle for every journey would be prohibitively expensive, and rather like building a new train for every journey between London and Bristol. This was the thinking behind the Space Shuttle, which may be said to take off like a rocket, fly like a space-ship, and land like a glider. Most of the components can be used over and over again, and the principle is sound enough, but unfortunately the technical problems proved to be much greater than had been expected, and the programme fell far behind schedule. Then, in 1986, came a tragedy when one of the Shuttles, Challenger, exploded soon after take-off, killing all the members of its crew. Even now it cannot be said that the Shuttles are wholly reliable, and following the collapse of the USSR we can only wait to see what will happen to the Russian shuttle, Buran.

It is now no longer a secret that the Russians aimed to be the first to put a man on the Moon; they failed because their launchers were not dependable enough. Yet they did send up the first automatic lunar probes, and in 1959 three were dispatched. Lunik 1 flew past the Moon, sending back useful data (such as the revelation that the Moon has no magnetic field); Lunik 2 crash-landed, and Lunik 3 went on a round trip, providing the first pictures of the far side of the Moon which is always turned away from the Earth. Next came their initial planetary probe, Venera 1, which was launched in February 1961. However, at that time the Russians were having major problems with long-range communication techniques. The probe probably passed quite close to Venus, but all contact with it had long since been lost, so that we will never know just what happened to it. The first success came in the following year, but it was American, not Russian; the target was again Venus.

Sending a probe to a planet is much more difficult than with the Moon. The Moon is our companion, and always stays close to us, but even Venus, the nearest of the planets, is always at least a hundred times as distant, and it orbits the Sun rather than the Earth. Moreover, it is not possible to wait until it is at its closest to us, and then simply fire a rocket across the gap; this would mean using fuel for the entire journey, and no space-craft could possibly carry enough. What we have to do is to make use of the Sun's gravity, and put the probe into what is termed a transfer orbit, so that it can 'coast' unpowered for most of the way.

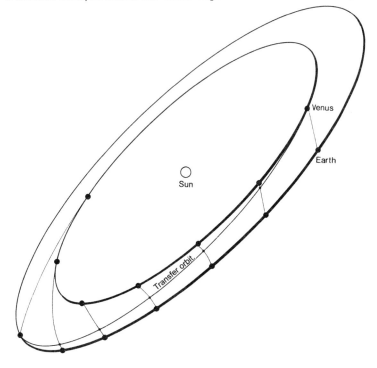

Transfer orbit

With an inner planet (i.e. Mercury or Venus) the probe has to be slowed down relative to the Earth. It will then start to swing inward toward the Sun, and the aim is to make it reach the orbit of the target planet at exactly the right moment. Mariner 2, the first of all successful interplanetary vehicles, was launched on 27 August 1962, and made its rendezvous with Venus on the following 14 December. (In case you are wondering what happened to Mariner 1, I have to tell you that it fell into the sea immediately after take-off; someone had forgotten to feed a minus sign into a computer.) Mariner 2 did not land, but simply by-passed Venus at a range of 21,000 miles, sending back valuable information before going on in a never-ending journey round the Sun; contact with it was finally lost in January 1963. Since then there have been many Venus probes, and the Russians have even made controlled landings there, obtaining pictures direct from the surface.

Mercury, the other inner planet, has been visited by just one space-craft: Mariner 10, which made three active passes in 1974 and 1975 and is still, no doubt, orbiting the Sun. Mariner 10 was the first probe to make use of what is termed the gravity-assist technique, since it passed Venus *en route* and used Venus' gravitational pull to put it into an orbit which took it on to a rendezvous with Mercury.

With a superior planet – that is to say, a planet further away from the Sun than we are – the procedure is to speed the space-craft up relative to the Earth, so that it will swing outward. Jupiter was the first target, with Pioneer 10, launched in March 1972; it made its pass of the Giant Planet in December of the following year. Pioneer 11 was an almost identical vehicle, sent up in 1973 and arriving in 1974, but after making its rendezvous with Jupiter it retained enough propellant for it to be swung back across the Solar System to an encounter with Saturn in 1979. But the Pioneers, good though they were, were upstaged by the Voyagers, both of which functioned flawlessly and both of which are still sending back signals.

Voyager 1 was dispatched in 1977, and passed Jupiter in 1979. It then used the gravity-assist technique to send it on to an encounter with Saturn, after which it began a never-ending journey out of the Solar System altogether. Its twin, Voyager 2, was even more ambitious. By a fortunate chance, during the late 1970s the four giant planets Jupiter, Saturn, Uranus and Neptune were strung out in a long, gentle curve, so that Voyager 2 was able to pass by them in turn – Jupiter in 1979, Saturn in 1981, Uranus in 1986 and Neptune in 1989. By the time it made its rendezvous with Neptune it had been in space for over twelve years and had covered more than four and a half thousand million miles – and yet it made its closest approach within two minutes of the scheduled time. (British Rail, please copy!)

This is no place to go into details of the space-craft themselves; it is enough to say that they were immensely complex. Although it is possible to use solar power in our part of the Solar System, this cannot be done at remote depths, because there is not enough sunlight; the Voyagers carried tiny nuclear generators, and they worked well. Of course, the amount of power sent back to Earth was minuscule, and would not have been enough to light up the bulb of a pocket torch for more than a fraction of a second, but electronic techniques can use this tiny pulse to produce the superb pictures which have told us so much about the outer planets.

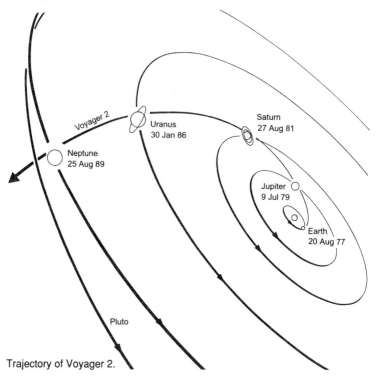

Trajectory of Voyager 2.

Of course there have been failures. The Russians have made no attempts to send probes beyond Mars, and even with Mars they have had no luck (which is surprising in view of their success with Venus, which should logically be a much more difficult target). The American programmes have been constantly hampered by cuts in funding – after all, a space-craft costs nearly as much as half a nuclear submarine! – and various important missions have had to be cancelled or at least drastically modified. What will happen in the immediate future remains to be seen, particularly with the chaotic situation in what used to be the Soviet Union, but it is no longer fantastic to talk about a permanent base on the Moon or a manned expedition to Mars.

This is a book about astronomy, not space research, but the two are now so closely intertwined that it is impossible to separate them, any more than one can separate arithmetic from algebra. I felt therefore that it was essential to say at least a little about the events following 4 October 1957; now let us return to the sky itself.

# 6

# THE SUN

More than a hundred years ago a famous populariser of astronomy, R. A. Proctor, wrote a book about the Sun. He subtitled it 'Ruler, Fire, Light and Life of the Planetary System', and with this nobody can disagree. Without the Sun we could not exist for a moment, and the Earth itself would never have come into existence. Yet it is only within the last two centuries that we have started to understand its nature, and there are still many important points about which we remain mystified. It has even been said that we know less about the Sun today than we thought we did at the beginning of the Space Age!

It is, of course, quite unlike the Earth or any planet. It is made of incandescent gas, and it is extremely hot. Even the visible surface is at a temperature of between 5000° and 6000° C, and at the core, where the solar energy is being produced, the temperature soars to the unbelievable value of at least 14,000,000° – perhaps more. The diameter of the globe is 865,000 miles, so that the Sun could swallow up over a million globes the volume of the Earth, but the mass is 'only' 330,000 times that of the Earth, because the density is much lower. In fact, the Sun 'weighs' only 1.4 times as much as an equal volume of water would do.

Attempts to find the distance between the Earth and the Sun were made in very early times, and although all these first efforts were very wide of the mark they were at least able to show that the Sun is a long way away. The best of the Greek estimates was that of Ptolemy, who put the Sun's distance at 5,000,000 miles, but the first reliable measurement was made in 1672 by the Italian astronomer

Sun and Earth compared

G. D. Cassini, who was at that time working in France as Director of the new Paris Observatory. Cassini's method involved using Kepler's Laws.

Kepler, remember, was the first to show that the planets move round the Sun in elliptical paths. His Third Law gave a definite relationship between the orbital period and the distance from the Sun; for instance, since he knew the orbital period of Mars (687 Earth days) and that of the Earth (in round figures 365 days) it was simple to show that Mars must be 1.52 times further away from the Sun than we are. Very well, then: find the actual distance of Mars, in miles, and that of the Earth can be found by straightforward mathematics. Therefore Cassini set out to find the distance of Mars, and he used the method of parallax, measuring the planet's position among the stars from sites on the Earth's surface as widely separated as possible.

His final result for the Earth-Sun distance, or astronomical unit, was 86,000,000 miles. Later measurements increased this to nearly 93,000,000 miles, and now we can use an entirely different method – that of radar.

Radar involves sending out a pulse of energy, bouncing it off a solid body (or equivalent) and then receiving the 'echo' or return signal. Radar pulses have been bounced off the planet Venus; we know how fast they travel, because their speed is the same as that of light (186,000 miles per second), and so the time taken for the pulse to travel from the Earth to Venus and back again gives us the distance of Venus. From this, the length of the astronomical unit can be worked out. It proves to be 92,976,000 miles (this is of course the mean distance, because the Earth's path round the Sun is not a perfect circle).

We know the Sun's distance; we know its size, and we know its temperature. We also know that its age must be rather greater than that of the Earth, which is around 4,600 million years. So how exactly does the Sun shine?

Some of the ideas current in the early and even mid nineteenth century were rather curious. Sir William Herschel, discoverer of Uranus, firmly believed that the brilliant solar surface lay above a calm, pleasant region which might well be inhabited – and he remained convinced of this throughout his lifetime (he died in 1822). Few people agreed with him, and it was tacitly assumed that the Sun must be burning in the manner of a vast bonfire. Unfortunately, rudimentary calculations showed that this could not be so. A Sun made up of coal, burning as fiercely as the real Sun actually does, would be reduced to ashes in less than five thousand years. Another idea was that the Sun's energy was due to constant peppering with particles coming from space, but this was found to be equally inadequate. The contraction theory proposed by H. von Helmholtz in 1834 was rather better; this time it was assumed that the Sun is shrinking by about 200 feet per year, releasing gravitational energy in the process. This would keep the Sun radiating for at least 15,000,000 years – but this again was not nearly long enough. The real solution came much later, and was based upon that all-important tool of the astronomer, the spectroscope.

We have seen that, just as a telescope collects light, so a spectroscope splits it up. Pass a beam of sunlight through a glass prism, as Newton did in 1666, and it will produce a rainbow band, from red at one end through orange, yellow, green and blue to violet at the other. This is

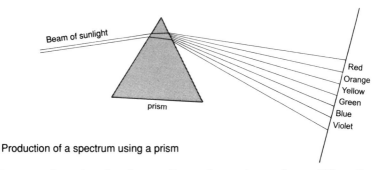

Production of a spectrum using a prism

because the prism bends or refracts the various colours differently: red least, violet most. It was in fact Newton who produced the first solar spectrum, though he never took his investigations much further.

The next step came in 1802 with the work of an Englishman, W. H. Wollaston. He passed sunlight through a slit, analysed it with a prism and saw that the rainbow band was crossed by dark lines. It was then that he missed scientific immortality. He thought that the lines merely marked the boundaries between the different colours, and did no more.

Next came a brilliant young German optician, Josef Fraunhofer, who had a romantic career; he was apprenticed to a Dickensian taskmaster, but when his ramshackle dwelling collapsed he was rescued and befriended by the Elector of Bavaria, who happened to be driving past in his coach. Subsequently Fraunhofer became the leader in his field, and it was he who, in 1814, went back to studies of the solar spectrum. Like Wollaston, he saw the dark lines. Unlike Wollaston, he realised that they were immensely significant. They always kept to the same positions, with the same intensities; he catalogued over 500 of them, and even today they are still often known as the Fraunhofer lines.

Unfortunately Fraunhofer died young, at the very height of his powers, and the dark lines were not explained until 1859, as a result of work mainly by Gustav Kirchhoff. Kirchhoff found that spectra are of two different types. An incandescent solid, liquid, or gas at high pressure will produce a continuous rainbow band from red at the long-wave end through to violet at the short-wave end. An incandescent gas at low pressure will yield disconnected bright lines, each of which is the trademark of some particular element or group of elements; for example, two prominent yellow lines in one position in the spectrum must be due to sodium. See those yellow lines, and you know that sodium is present.

The Sun's bright surface or photosphere produces a continuous spec-

Solar spectrum

Absorption or Fraunhofer lines

trum. Above it is a region of much more rarefied gas, termed the chromosphere, which should yield a bright-line or emission spectrum; but when seen against the rainbow background, the lines are 'reversed', and appear dark. This does not affect their positions or their intensities. Look at the yellow part of the band, and you will see two conspicuous dark lines. These lines correspond exactly to the familiar bright yellow lines of sodium, and we can prove that there is sodium in the Sun.

Some elements produce very complicated spectra (thousands of lines in the case of iron, for example), but by now most of the 92 naturally-occurring elements have been tracked down in the Sun. Helium, the second lightest of all the elements, was found in the solar spectrum years before it was isolated on Earth, and this accounts for its name – *helios* is Greek for 'Sun'. The English astronomer Norman Lockyer found it in the Sun in 1868, and not until 1894 was it identified on Earth.

All in all, we can now tell 'what the Sun is made of'. It is interesting to recall that in 1830 the French philosopher Auguste Comte stated that the chemistry of the stars was something which Mankind could never find out. This proves, surely, that when a French philosopher makes a profound statement he is almost certain to be wrong ...

The main constituent of the Sun is hydrogen, and this is no surprise, because hydrogen is the commonest element in the entire universe; indeed, atoms of hydrogen outnumber the atoms of all other elements put together. For every million hydrogen atoms in the Sun there are 63,000 of helium; next comes oxygen, with less than 700. So hydrogen accounts for 71 per cent of the Sun by mass, helium 27 per cent, and all the other elements combined less than 2 per cent.

Now we can start to investigate the way in which the Sun produces its energy; we have to deal with nuclear reactions near the core, where the temperatures and pressures are so high. For a while it was thought that the energy was due to atoms literally annihilating each other, but on this theory the Sun could last for millions of millions of years, giving a timescale which was as obviously too long as the contraction-theory timescale had been obviously too short. The basic process was worked out in 1938 almost simultaneously by two scientists, Hans Bethe in America and George Gamow in Europe. Bethe had been attending a conference in Washington, and was returning to his university by train when he started to think about the solar energy problem; by the time he drew into his home station he had broken the back of the main puzzle!

Hydrogen is the key, and acts as the Sun's 'fuel'. At the core, the nuclei of hydrogen atoms are running together to make up the nuclei of the next lightest element, helium. It takes four hydrogen nuclei to produce one nucleus of helium, and every time this happens a little energy is set free and a little mass is lost, because the newly-created helium nucleus 'weighs' slightly less than the original four hydrogen nuclei combined. It is this released energy which keeps the Sun shining, and the loss in mass amounts to 4,000,000 tons per second. This sounds alarming, but the Sun is so massive that by solar standards the loss is trifling, and there is enough 'fuel' to maintain the Sun in more or less its present state for several thousands of millions of years yet.

Of course, the supply of hydrogen will not last indefinitely, and in the long run it will become exhausted. When this happens, the Sun will have to change its structure. The core will shrink and become even hotter, while the outer layers will swell out as different reactions begin. The Sun will become a red giant star, and this is certain to mean the end of the Earth, so that our world has a limited lifetime, and if Mankind still survives in that far-off period it will be time to consider migrating to a safer home! The Sun will then shed its outer layers altogether, and the remaining core will become very small and amazingly dense, glowing feebly as a 'white dwarf' star before losing the last of its light and heat and ending up as a cold, dead globe. I will have more to say about stellar evolution later, but at least we may be sure that nothing drastic is likely to happen yet awhile.

On the other hand, the Sun is variable to some extent, and this is shown by the behaviour of the dark patches known as sunspots.

The bright solar surface, or photosphere, is generally disturbed by one or more of these patches. They have been known ever since they were studied with telescopes, from 1609 onward, and occasional spots visible with the naked eye were recorded from Ancient China, but of course their nature was unknown, and it was often supposed that they were openings in the bright photosphere, revealing darker, cooler material beneath. However, we now know that they are essentially magnetic phenomena. The Sun does have a magnetic field, and the lines of force run from one magnetic pole to the other, not very far below the surface of the photosphere. When the lines break through to the surface itself they temporarily cool it, and a sunspot results. In most cases a spot-group consists of two main outbreaks, which, predictably, have opposite magnetic polarity.

The Sun rotates on its axis – not as a solid body would do, because the equatorial region rotates faster than the poles; the equatorial period is 25 days, the polar period 34 days (this sort of behaviour is known as differential rotation). A sunspot will be carried slowly across the Earth-turned disk, and eventually it will vanish over the limb, to reappear a fortnight or so later, assuming that it has not disappeared in the meantime. No spot-group lasts for very long. A major group may persist for some months, but single small spots may have lifetimes of only a few hours.

A century and half ago, a German apothecary named Heinrich Schwabe was making daily observations of the Sun when he discovered something very interesting. There is a roughly regular solar cycle. Every eleven years the Sun is active, with many spots and spotgroups; activity then dies down, and at minimum there may be many consecutive days with no spots at all, after which the groups become more common again up to the time of the next maximum. Thus there were maxima in 1958, 1969, 1980,1991; in the mid-1980s and mid-1990s activity was very low indeed.

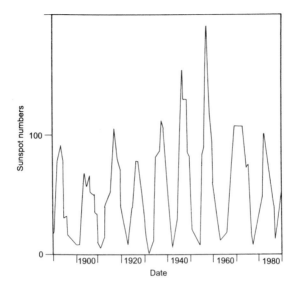

Solar cycle. Sunspot numbers over 100-year period, 1880–1980

It was then found that there is another law, this time relating to the latitudes of the spots. The first spots of a new cycle appear at fairly high solar latitudes; later outbreaks appear closer to the Sun's equator, though they never actually break out on the equator itself. Even before the last low-latitude spots of the old cycle die out, we see the first spots of the new cycle appearing at higher latitudes. This is known as Spörer's Law, after the German who was one of the first to draw attention to it. The polarities of two-spot groups are also affected by the cycle. Suppose that in the Sun's northern hemisphere the 'leader' is a north-polarity spot and the 'follower' south-polarity; this will apply to all northern-hemisphere groups, while in the southern hemisphere it is the leader which will have south-polarity. At the end of the cycle there is a full reversal, so that it may even be said that the true length of a cycle is not 11 years, but 22.

The cycle is not perfectly regular, and the eleven-year interval between one maximum and the next is merely an average. Moreover, it seems that between 1645 and 1715 there were almost no spots at all, so that the cycle was suspended; this is known as the Maunder Minimum, because the English astronomer E. W. Maunder was one of the first to note it by examination of the old records. We cannot be sure that spots were completely absent, because the records are so incomplete, but it does seem that they were rare, and there is also some evidence of earlier spot-free periods.

Whether the solar cycle has any direct effect upon the Earth's climate is a matter for debate. It may or may not be significant that the Maunder Minimum coincided with what has been called the Little Ice Age in Europe; in England, for example, the Thames froze almost every winter during the 1680s, and frost fairs were held on it, while there was serious talk of evacuating Iceland altogether. But it would be idle to pretend that we really know, and neither can we claim to have a full knowledge of exactly how the Sun functions, though we believe we are on the right track.

A large spot consists of a dark central portion or umbra, surrounded by a lighter area or penumbra. (In fact, no spot is really dark; it appears so only because it is around 2000° cooler than the surrounding photosphere. If it could be seen shining on its own, it would be intensely brilliant.) Some spots are regular in outline, but others are not, and there may be many umbrae contained in a single mass of penumbra, while single spots are also common. When a spot nears the Sun's limb it appears foreshortened, and from this it seems that most spots – not all – are depressions; the penumbra is always narrowest

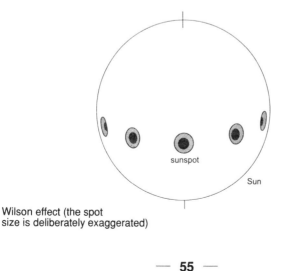

sunspot

Sun

Wilson effect (the spot
size is deliberately exaggerated)

toward the limb, as was pointed out by the Scottish astronomer A. Wilson as long ago as 1774. Not all spots show the Wilson effect, but it is always worth looking for.

Other features of the photosphere include *faculae* (Latin, 'torches'), which are bright areas usually associated with spot-groups, and are made up of high-level incandescent gases; they are best seen near the limb, where the photosphere is less brilliant than at the centre of the disk, and spectroscope analysis shows that they are made up of hydrogen. The surface also has a granular structure; each granule is around 6000 miles across, and has a lifetime of about eight minutes. It has been estimated that the entire surface contains about 4,000,000 granules at any one time, so that the Sun is never calm even when at the minimum of its cycle.

Active spot-groups may produce short-lived, violent outbreaks known as flares, which send out electrified particles as well as short-wave radiations; it is these particles which cross the 93-million-mile gap between the Sun and the Earth and cascade down into the upper air, producing the lovely glows known as aurorae or polar lights. Flare activity may also interfere with layers in our upper atmosphere, and cause problems with radio reception. But few flares can be seen in visible light, so that most have to be studied with equipment based upon the principle of the spectroscope. Basically, what is done is to use a filter or equivalent device to cut out the light of all wavelengths except that of hydrogen or another selected element, such as calcium; flares and associated phenomena then become striking.

Observing the Sun is a fascinating pastime, but it can be very danger- ous indeed, and there are traps for the unwary. Remember, the Sun is very hot indeed. Look straight at it through any telescope or pair of binoculars, and you will focus all the light and heat on to your eye, with tragic results. Using a dark filter in this way is emphatically not to be recommended, because the filter is always liable to shatter with- out warning, and in any case will not give full protection. It is sad but true that many people have blinded themselves permanently by using telescopes to look at the Sun, and I have known two cases myself. The only sensible method is to point the telescope at the Sun without look- ing through it, and then project the solar image on to a white screen, held or fixed behind the eyepiece. True, there are some 'wedges' which are harmless enough, but my advice is never to use them unless you have expert guidance. In any case, projecting the image gives

Projecting the Sun

satisfactory results, and it is easy to make daily plots of the groups as they cross the disk from one limb to the other. You can also work out what is called the daily Zürich number, calculated by the formula $R = k(10g + f)$, where $R$ is the Zürich number, $g$ is the number of separate groups on view, and $f$ is the number of separate umbrae. $k$ is a constant depending upon the observer's equipment and experience, but it is usually close to unity. These are also known as Wolf numbers, as the system was devised by R. Wolf of Zürich in 1852.

Above the photosphere we have the chromosphere or 'coloursphere', and beyond this again comes the Sun's outer atmosphere, called the corona. Spectroscopic equipment can show the chromosphere and associated phenomena at any time, but for a good view of the corona we must either take a trip into space or else wait for a total solar eclipse.

During its monthly orbit round the Earth, there must obviously be times when the Moon passes directly between the Earth and the Sun. It so happens that the Sun and the Moon appear almost exactly the same size in the sky; the Sun's diameter is 400 times that of the Moon, but it is also 400 times further away. This is sheer coincidence – it can be nothing else – but it is fortunate for us.

Solar eclipses are of three types: partial, total and annular. During a partial eclipse only a limited area of the Sun is hidden and although

Theory of a solar eclipse

it makes for an interesting spectacle it is not particularly striking. Neither is an annular eclipse, when the lining-up is exact but the Moon is at or near the furthest part of its orbit round the Earth; it does not then look quite large enough to cover the Sun, so that a ring of the photosphere is left showing round the dark disk of the Moon (hence the name: Latin *annulus,* a ring). However, a total eclipse is dramatic by any standards, and may well lay claim to being the most glorious sight in all Nature. As the last sliver of the photosphere is hidden by the advancing disk of the Moon, the Sun's atmosphere flashes into sight; we see the chromosphere, with the red masses of hydrogen which used to be called Red Flames but are now known as prominences, and also the marvellous pearly corona, which stretches out from the Sun in all directions.

The chromosphere, lying directly above the photosphere, is the region where the Fraunhofer lines are produced; in it we find the prominences, which may be either relatively quiescent or else violently eruptive. They are not always present, but at most total eclipses at least one or two are seen. (Incidentally, it was only after the eclipse of 1852 that astronomers finally became certain that they were solar rather than lunar, which shows how little we knew about the Sun a hundred and fifty years ago!) Because we can study the prominences with spectroscopic equipment at any time, without waiting for an eclipse, we know how they behave; but the corona is much more elusive, and this is why scientists are still willing to go on long journeys to make the most of a few fleeting seconds of totality.

The corona is made up of gas, chiefly hydrogen. Its density is very low – less than one million-millionth of that of the Earth's air at sea-level – but its temperature is very high, and rises to almost 2,000,000°. From this one might imagine that it emits a tremendous amount of heat, but nothing could be further from the truth. Scientifically, 'temperature' is defined by the rate at which the various atoms and molecules move around; the faster the speeds, the higher the temperature. In the corona the speeds are very great, but there are so few particles that the actual 'heat' is negligible. We are still not sure why the coronal temperature is so high, but on the whole it seems likely that once again we are dealing with some sort of magnetic phenomenon.

Unfortunately, the Moon's shadow is only just long enough to touch the Earth, and so eclipses as seen from any one particular locality are relatively rare. If the orbits of the Earth and the Moon lay in the same plane, we would have a solar eclipse at every new moon, but in fact the lunar orbit is inclined to ours at an angle of just over five degrees, so that on most occasions the new moon passes unseen either above or below the Sun in the sky. To produce an eclipse, the new moon must be very near a node – a node being the point where the Moon's path cuts the plane of the ecliptic. Moreover, a total eclipse is a rushed affair; it can never last for as long as eight minutes, and is generally much briefer. To either side of the zone of totality there is, of course, a partial eclipse.

It so happens that the Sun, the Moon and the nodes arrive back at almost the same relative positions in a period of approximately 18 years 11 days, known as the Saros, so that any eclipse is quite likely to be followed by another eclipse 18 years 11 days later. The conditions are not identical, but the Saros is a reasonable guide, and was good enough for the ancients to make predictions. Thus Thales of Miletus was able to forecast the eclipse of 25 May 585 BC, which is said to have stopped a battle between the armies of the Lydians and Medes; the combatants were so alarmed at the sudden darkness that they concluded a hasty peace. Not that the sky is completely dark during totality; it is not, but it becomes dusky enough for planets and bright stars to be seen.

There are many phenomena associated with total eclipses – for example Baily's Beads, bright points seen just before and just after totality when the sunlight passes through valleys on the Moon's limb. Then there are shadow bands, wavy lines on the Earth's surface also seen just before and just after totality.

All in all, there is nothing to rival the glory of a total eclipse; if you have the chance of seeing one, do not hesitate. Stay in England, and you must wait until 11 August 1999, when the track will cross Cornwall (the last English totality dates back to 1927), but there will be a total eclipse before then on 26 February 1998, lasting for 3 minutes 14 seconds. It will be seen from the Indian Ocean to the Pacific.

It is no surprise to find that the Sun sends out radiations at all wavelengths. Studies of solar X-rays have to be carried out from space vehicles, and these methods have been invaluable; for instance we can now track the so-called 'coronal holes', regions of exceptionally low density in the corona, which are important because they provide escape routes for the solar wind – made up of streams of low-energy particles sent out by the Sun all the time. There have been special probes such as Ulysses, which was put into a path enabling it to study the poles of the Sun, which we can never examine properly from Earth because we see them at such an unfavourable angle. The polar regions are of special significance, because it is here that the lines of the Sun's magnetic field are open rather than closed, making it easier for the solar wind particles to break free. Predictably, the Sun is also a strong source of radio waves, and here at least a great deal of research can be carried out from ground level.

Finally, it is worth saying something about a problem which has been puzzling astronomers for years – and still does. Theory predicts that as the Sun radiates, it should release vast numbers of particles known as neutrinos, which are excessively difficult to detect because they have no electrical charge and virtually no mass – perhaps none at all. Deep in Homestake gold-mine in South Dakota, Ray Davies and his team have built what is certainly the world's strangest 'telescope'. It consists of a large tank of over 460,000 litres of cleaning fluid, and it is buried in a disused mine-shaft a mile below ground. The fluid is rich in chlorine, and it is known that if a neutrino scores a direct hit on a chlorine nucleus it can change the chlorine into a special form of another gas, argon, which is easy to identify. The mile-deep location is essential because if the experiment were set up on or near the Earth's surface it would be wrecked by other particles, known (misleadingly) as cosmic rays, which are bombarding us from all directions all the time, and would produce the same effects. Luckily, the cosmic rays cannot penetrate down to Davies' tank of cleaning fluid.

The results have been startling: far fewer neutrinos have been detected than had been anticipated. There is nothing wrong with the experiment, which in any case has now been duplicated elsewhere, and so there must be something wrong with our theories. As yet the problem remains unsolved, and it is a salutary reminder that we do not know nearly as much about the Sun as we would like to do.

Always remember, too, that the Sun is the only star which is sufficiently close to us to be examined in great detail, so that it is the main key in our quest for knowledge of the other stars. Solar physics has become one of the most vital branches of modern astronomy, and there are many observatories which concentrate solely upon it. We have come a long way since William Herschel claimed that the Sun is a cool, habitable world.

# 7
# THE MOON

Just as the Sun rules the day, so the Moon is dominant at night, at least for part of every month; full moonlight can appear so brilliant that it is not always easy to appreciate that it would take roughly half a million full moons to equal the light of the Sun. Yet the amount of heat sent to us from the Moon is negligible, so that it is quite safe to look straight at it through a telescope or binoculars. (Recently there has been a report of eye damage due to staring at the full moon through a telescope. I admit to being somewhat sceptical about this; in any case there can be no problem at all unless you deliberately stare for a very long time – and the same could be said of looking straight at a searchlight. It is, surely, a question of common sense.)

Imposing though it looks, the Moon is a very junior member of the Sun's family. It is smaller than the Earth, with a diameter of only 2158 miles, and it has only 1/81 of the Earth's mass, so that its gravitational pull is much weaker; the escape velocity is a mere 1½ miles

Earth and Moon compared

per second, so that the Moon has been unable to hold on to any atmosphere it may once have had, and is today airless, waterless and lifeless. The dark patches still called 'seas' have never had any water in them, though it is true that they were once oceans of liquid lava.

We cannot be sure about the origin of the Moon. The old idea that it simply broke away from a rapidly spinning Earth has been given up – mathematically, it is untenable – and there are also difficulties in assuming that it was once an independent body which came too close to the Earth and was unable to break free again. There is growing support for the idea that at an early stage in the evolution of the Solar System there was a collision between the Earth and a large wandering body, hurling around a vast amount of debris which then collected to form the Moon. At least we know that the two bodies are of much the same age; the rocks brought home by the Apollo astronauts and the automatic Russian probes show that both are of the same vintage.

It is often said that 'the Moon moves round the Earth'. This is true enough, but there is one modification, because strictly speaking the Earth and Moon move together round the barycentre, which is the common centre of gravity of the system. But since the Earth is 81 times as massive as the Moon, the barycentre lies deep inside the terrestrial globe, and the simple statement is good enough to satisfy anyone except a mathematician. The lunar orbit is not circular; the distance from Earth ranges between 221,460 miles at its closest (perigee) out to 252,700 miles at its furthest (apogee).

The orbital period is 27.3 days. The cause of the regular phases, or apparent changes of shape, is easy to explain. When the Moon is more or less between the Earth and the Sun, its dark or night side is facing us, and we cannot see it at all – except when the alignment is exact, and we have a solar eclipse (as we have noted, this does not happen every month, because of the 5-degree tilt of the Moon's path). This, and not the slender crescent seen soon afterwards in the evening sky, is the true new moon. In position 2 in the diagram half the sunlit side faces us; rather confusingly this is known as First Quarter, because the Moon has then completed one-quarter of its journey. In position 3 we see the whole of the sunlit face (full moon) and in position 4, half again (Last Quarter). Between half and full the Moon is said to be gibbous. Because the Earth and the Moon are moving together round the Sun, the interval between one new moon and the next, known as the synodic period, is 29 1/2 days rather than just over 27; the diagram should make this clear.

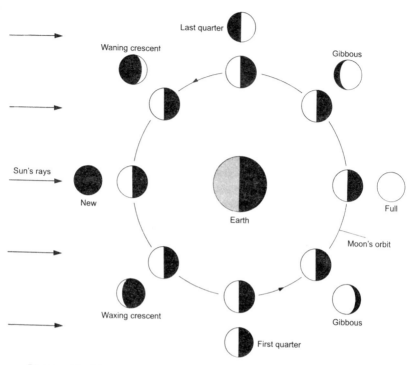

Phases of the Moon

When the Moon is in the crescent stage, the night side can often be seen shining faintly. This is due to light reflected on to the Moon from the Earth, and is therefore known as the earthshine. Its cause has been known for a long time; Leonardo da Vinci may have been the first to explain it. Country folk call it 'the Old Moon in the Young Moon's arms'. And while on the subject of country lore, it is worth adding that so far as we can tell, the Moon has absolutely no effect on the weather. Quite apart from anything else, new moon and perigee do not often coincide; there is no reason why they should.

The Moon is a slow spinner. Our rotation period is 24 hours; that of the Moon is 27.3 days – exactly the same as its orbital period. This may sound a strange coincidence, but there is a straightforward explanation for it. Initially the Earth and the Moon were viscous, and raised tides in each other. The tides raised by the Earth on the Moon were much the more powerful, because of the Earth's greater mass, and the effect was to slow the Moon's rotation down as it span; the Earth tried to keep a 'bulge' pointing in our direction. Eventually the rotation had stopped altogether relative to the Earth – but not relative to the Sun, so that on the Moon's surface day and night conditions are the same everywhere. A lunar day is almost as long as two Earth weeks.

It follows that the same side of the Moon is always turned toward us, and that there is part of the surface which we can never see – a fact which used to infuriate pre-Space Age observers (such as myself). However, things are not quite so bad as they might seem. Though the Moon turns on its axis at a constant speed, it does not move round us at a constant speed; following Kepler's Laws, it moves quickest when closest-in. Each month, therefore, the position in orbit and the amount of spin become out of step, and we can peer a little way round alternate mean limbs. This, together with other less important effects of the same kind, known as librations, means that altogether we can examine a grand total of 59 per cent of the whole of the surface; it is only 41 per cent which is permanently hidden. With the circumlunar flight of the unmanned Russian spacecraft Lunik 3, in 1959, we had

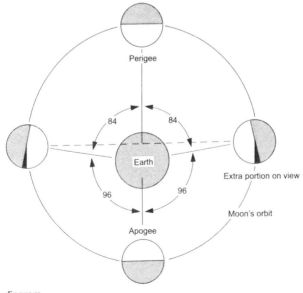

Libration diagram

our first direct view of the Moon's far side. Predictably, it proved to be essentially similar to the areas which we have always known, though there were differences in detail.

The main effect of the Moon upon the Earth concerns the tides. As a start, let us imagine that the whole Earth is covered with a shallow uniform ocean, and that both the Earth and the Moon are standing still. In the diagram, which is not to scale, we will have a high tide at point A and another high tide at point B, with low tides at C and D; the Moon's gravity is heaping the water up at A, where the pull is strongest. Of course the solid land is being pulled as well, but land is much more difficult to shift than water, so that the heaping-up is less.

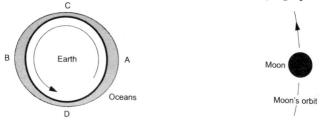

Tides

This is all very well, but why should there also be a high tide at B? It is slightly misleading to say simply that the solid globe is being 'pulled away' from the water, so for the moment let us assume that we have a situation in which the Earth and the Moon are absolutely alone in the universe, and are falling toward each other. Point A, which is closest to the Moon, will be subject to a greater accelerating force than the average, and so the water will be bunched upward. At B, the reverse will happen. The acceleration will be less than average, so that the water in that region will tend to be 'left behind', bulging away from the Moon and producing a similar high tide.

Next, assume that the Earth and the Moon are keeping the same distance apart, but that the Earth is spinning round once in 24 hours. Obviously the water-heaps will not spin with it; they will try to keep 'under' the Moon. Therefore, each bulge will sweep round the Earth once a day, so that every region will have two high tides and two low tides in each 24 hours.

However, there are many complications. First, the Earth is not covered with a uniform water-shell, and the outlines of the seas and continents play a very major role. Secondly, the Moon is moving along in its orbit, so that the water-heaps shift slowly as they follow the Moon around. Also, the waters take time to heap up, so that the maximum tide does not fall directly below the Moon; there is an appreciable lag. All in all, tidal phenomena are surprisingly complicated.

Neither can we neglect the Sun, which also raises tides. They are much weaker than those of the Moon, because the Sun is 400 times as remote, and the main tide-raising force is due to the difference in pull on opposite sides of the Earth. When the Sun and Moon are pulling in the same sense, at new or full moon, the tides are strongest (spring tides; the term has nothing to do with the season of spring), while when the Sun and Moon are pulling against each other, at half-moon, we have the weaker neap tides. Anyone who lives on the coast, as I do, will be very conscious of the difference in strength.

I appreciate that this account of tidal phenomena is hopelessly over-simplified, but to go into real detail would take many pages, so let us now turn to the lunar world itself.

Even a casual glance at the Moon will show the light and dark areas; who has not heard of the Man in the Moon? It is said that the patterns do give a vague impression of a human form, though I admit that I have never myself been able to make it out. Originally it was thought that the bright areas were land and the dark areas water; we still use romantic names such as the Sea of Tranquillity, the Bay of Dews and the Ocean of Storms, though at an early stage in the telescopic era it was realised that the so-called seas are bone-dry. The Latin names are always used; thus the Sea of Tranquillity becomes the Mare Tranquillitatis, the Bay of Dews is Sinus Roris, and so on.

Some of the seas or *maria* are fairly regular in form; the largest of these, the Mare Imbrium (Sea of Showers) is bounded in part by high mountain ranges, the Lunar Apennines and Alps. Ranges are often given terrestrial names, and some of the peaks are lofty, rising to well over 20,000 feet; there are also many isolated hills and mountains. Level country is very rare on the Moon.

Of course the whole scene is dominated by the craters, which range from huge enclosures well over 150 miles across down to tiny pits at the limit of visibility as seen from Earth. Many of the craters have terraced walls, together with central mountains or groups of mountains; thus the superb Theophilus, at the edge of the Mare Nectaris (Sea of Nectar) is 64 miles across and has a massive central mountain complex. The highest peaks on the wall-crest tower to 18,000 feet above the deepest part of the sunken floor, but to a much lower height above the outer surface, and in fact a lunar crater seen in profile

Profile of lunar crater

would resemble a shallow saucer much more than a steep-sided well. Neither does a central peak ever attain the height of the outer rampart, and it is probably apt to call a lunar crater a sunken plain, though there is one formation, the 54-mile Wargentin, which is lava-filled and takes the form of a plateau.

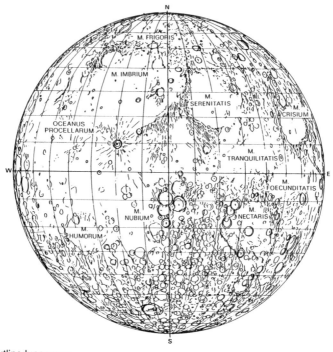

Outline lunar map

The craters were named by the Italian astronomer Riccioli, who drew a lunar map in 1651. His method was to christen craters after famous persons, usually (though not always) astronomers. The system has been followed through to the present day, and has been extended, but naturally Riccioli 'used up' all the main craters, so that later astronomers such as Newton and Herschel have had to make do with second best. Galileo is represented by a very obscure crater in the Oceanus Procellarum, but this was deliberate; Riccioli had no faith in the Copernican system, and, in his own words, 'flung Galileo into the Ocean of Storms'. However, Riccioli did relent sufficiently to give Copernicus one of the most splendid formations on the Moon. It lies in the Mare Nubium (Sea of Clouds); it is well-formed, 56 miles across with superbly terraced walls, and near full moon it is seen to be the focal point of a system of bright streaks or rays which stretch out for long distances in all directions. There is an even more extensive ray-centre in the southern uplands of the Moon, issuing from the crater named in honour of Tycho Brahe. The rays are surface deposits; they cast no shadows, and are well seen only when the Sun is high above them.

Not all craters are similar to Tycho and Copernicus. For example Plato, which is 60 miles across and lies in the uplands between the Mare Frigoris (Sea of Cold) and the Mare Imbrium, has an iron-grey floor which is almost devoid of detail. Though it is circular, it is well away from the apparent centre of the Moon's disk, and is drawn out into the shape of an ellipse. All craters near the limb are foreshortened, and in the libration regions – that is to say, the areas which are periodically tipped in and out of view – it is often difficult to distinguish a crater-wall from a ridge. Before the coming of the space probes, maps of these regions were of low accuracy.

Minor features of the Moon include domes, which are low swellings often crowned by summit pits; ridges, some of which snake across the maria; valleys, and cracklike features known as rills, rilles or clefts, some of which are prominent enough to be seen with very small telescopes. Many of them are in part crater-chains, though others are fairly obviously collapse features, and look superficially like cracks in dried mud.

The distribution of the craters is not random; when one formation breaks into another it is almost always the smaller crater which intrudes into the larger. There are pairs of craters, groups, and chains of vast formations which are clearly of different ages. Some craters have been so broken and distorted that they are barely recognisable, and this applies also to some of the major walled plains; for example

Bailly, in the far south, is more than 180 miles in diameter, but has been fittingly described as 'a field of ruins'.

How were the craters formed? This is a question which has led to endless arguments. The popular view nowadays is that they were produced by a violent natural bombardment between 3900 and 3200 million years ago, when meteorites thudded down on to the lunar surface and left their scars. The alternative view – that the main craters are of volcanic origin – has fallen into disfavour, though it still has some supporters (including myself). At any rate, nothing much has happened on the Moon for a very long time, and the main activity ended at least 3000 million years ago, so that even a 'young' crater such as Tycho or Copernicus is very ancient by terrestrial standards, and the dinosaurs must have seen the Moon very much as it is now. The only traces of current activity are very mild, localised gaseous emissions from below the crust.

I have already said something about the space missions, which began with the automatic Russian Luniks of 1959 and were followed by the U.S. Surveyors and Orbiters, further Russian unmanned missions, and then of course the Apollo landings, culminating in the touchdown of the *Eagle*, from Apollo 11, in July 1969. I doubt whether anyone has bettered Buzz Aldrin's description of the lunar scene as 'magnificent desolation'. The sky is black even in the daytime; there is no 'weather', and no sound. The flags set up by the astronauts do not flutter; how could they, in the absence of wind? Various artifacts left on the surface will not deteriorate; there are various crashed spacecraft, the bottom stages of Apollo modules, three 'Moon cars' in which the astronauts of Apollos 15, 16 and 17 drove themselves around, and of course the scientific recording instruments, now (sadly) switched off for reasons of economy. No doubt all these will be collected in due course and taken off to lunar museums ... And there is nothing far-fetched about a Lunar Base. If we wanted to do so, we could probably build it within the next couple of decades, and it would be of immense value, not least as a medical research centre. Meanwhile, the Moon has been more or less neglected since the end of the Apollo programme in 1972, though in 1994 a small photographic probe, Clementine – named after the character in the old mining song who is 'lost and gone forever' – proved to be very successful. In particular, Clementine surveyed the lunar poles, and it has been suggested that there is ice inside some of the craters whose floors are permanently in shadow, so that they are bitterly cold. I have grave reservations about this, but we must await the results of further research.

Telescopically, the lunar aspect changes with bewildering rapidity, not because it actually does so but because of the changing angle of sunlight. When a crater is near the terminator, or boundary between the daylit and night hemispheres, it is wholly or partly shadow-filled, and may be very prominent; near full moon the shadows virtually vanish, and the scene is dominated by the bright ray systems, mainly those of Tycho and Copernicus, so that even large walled plains may be hard to identify unless they are exceptionally bright or exceptionally dark. Plato is always recognisable because of the greyness of its floor, and so are Grimaldi and Riccioli near the western limb, while the 23-mile crater Aristarchus, in the Oceanus Procellarum, is so brilliant that unwary observers have mistaken it for a volcano in eruption. It does not take long to learn your way around the lunar surface, but remember that the best views are obtained during the crescent, half and gibbous phases; full moon is the very worst time for the beginner to start observing.

When the Moon is full, it may sometimes pass into the shadow cast by the Earth, and the result is a lunar eclipse; this does not happen every month, again because of the 5-degree tilt of the Moon's orbit. Lunar eclipses may be either total or partial, and are commoner than solar eclipses as seen from any particular site – because an eclipse of the Moon can be seen from any place where the Moon is above the horizon, whereas to see an eclipse of the Sun you have to be in just the right place at just the right time. It cannot be said that a lunar eclipse is spectacular, but it is well worth watching; the supply of direct sunlight is cut off, and the Moon becomes dim and often coppery until it passes out of the shadow again. In general it does not disappear completely, because some of the Sun's rays are bent on to it by way of the shell of atmosphere surrounding the Earth, but everything depends on conditions in the upper air, through which all the sunlight reaching the eclipsed Moon has to pass. When the upper regions are laden with dust and ash – as for example in the months following the recent eruption of Mount Pinotubo, in the Philippines – the eclipse may be so 'dark' that the Moon is difficult to find at all; at other eclipses there are lovely colours, and there is great scope for photographers, particularly as a lunar eclipse is a comparatively leisurely affair. Totality may last for well over an hour.

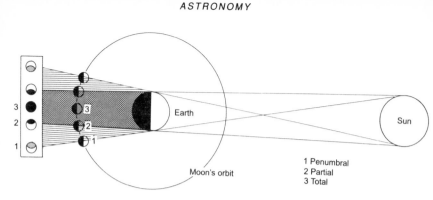

Theory of lunar eclipse

The next total eclipse is that of 16 September 1997. After that we must wait until 21 January 2000 and 9 January 2001.

There are also times when the Moon passes in front of a star, and hides or occults it. Because of the lack of lunar atmosphere, the star shines steadily until the instant when it is covered up by the advancing limb, when it snaps out as suddenly as a candle-flame in the wind. Planets can also be occulted now and then, though here the immersion and emersion are gradual, because a planet appears as a disk rather than a point source of light.

After Apollo, there seemed to be a general feeling that we had learned all that we wanted to know about the Moon, and that there was little point in studying it further. This is quite wrong. There are still many problems to be cleared up, and in any case the Moon has lost none of its magic; it is our faithful companion in space, and our skies would indeed be dull without it.

# 8
# THE
# SUN'S FAMILY

There was a time, not so very long ago, when it was generally thought that the Solar System was unique, or at least so exceptional that the chances of finding 'other Earths' in the Galaxy was minimal. Nowadays we think differently, because our theories have changed.

Much depends upon how the planets were formed. Initially there was great support for the so-called Nebular Hypothesis, proposed by the great French scientist Laplace in the 1790s. He assumed that the system began as a rotating gas-cloud, which shrank under the influence of gravitation; regular rings were thrown off, each one of which condensed into a planet, while the central part of the cloud became the Sun. However, there were so many mathematical objections that the idea was abandoned, and was replaced by a crop of 'tidal theories', of which the most celebrated was championed by Sir James Jeans, a well-known populariser of astronomy during the inter-war years (he was also a leading astrophysicist, and only in his later career did he change over to writing books for beginners). According to Jeans, the planets were pulled off the Sun by the action of a passing star; a cigar-shaped tongue of material was produced, and this broke up to form the planets. Predictably, the largest planets, Jupiter and Saturn, are in the middle of the system, where the thickest part of the cigar would have been.

If this had been valid, then Solar Systems would have been vanishingly rare, because the stars are so widely spaced that close approaches seldom occur, and it would have been quite likely that our planetary system would have been the only one in the Galaxy. But again the

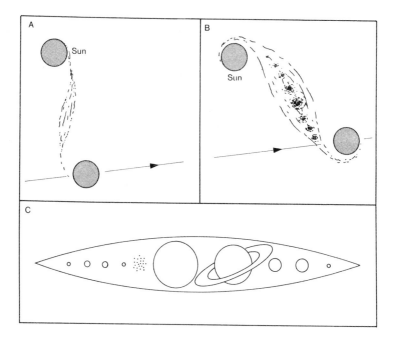

Jeans' tidal theory. Star passes close to Sun, pulling material from it (diagrams A and B). Planets form from this material (diagram C)

mathematicians swarmed to the attack, and eventually the tidal theory joined Laplace's gaseous rings on the scientific scrap-heap.

Nowadays we have a much more plausible theory, which, ironically, is closer to Laplace's than to Jeans'. The planets are assumed to have condensed out of a cloud of material associated with the youthful Sun, so that they are of very similar age. This explains why the Solar System is divided so sharply into two parts. Close to the Sun the temperatures where high, so that light gases such as hydrogen and helium were driven away, and the inner planets were left with only the heavier elements. Further out the temperatures were lower, so that the lightest elements could be retained – which is why the giants, unlike the inner members of the system, are not solid and rocky. True, a giant planet may have a solid core, but most of their globes are liquid, with deep atmospheres rich in hydrogen and helium.

Though the planets shine only by borrowed sunlight, their reflecting powers or albedoes are very different. Thus cloud-covered Venus reflects about 76 per cent of the sunlight falling on it, while the albedo of rocky Mercury is a mere 6 per cent (much the same as the average albedo of the Moon). And because the planets are of very different sizes, and lie at very different distances from us, they show a wide range in brilliancy. The first five must have been known from the dawn of human history; Venus and Jupiter are always much brighter than any of the stars, and so is Mars at its best, while Saturn is prominent enough, and even Mercury can be quite conspicuous. The ancients knew Mercury well, even though initially they believed that the 'evening Mercury' and the 'morning Mercury' were two different bodies – an error also made with regard to Venus.

A table summarising the main planetary data is given in Appendix 1, but perhaps a scale model will be useful here, so let us represent the

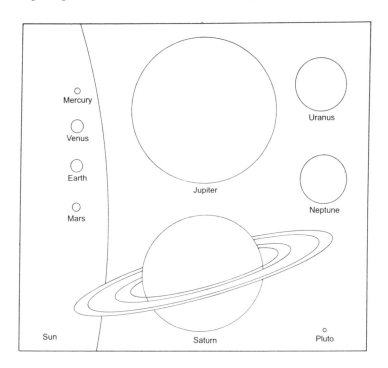

Sizes of the planets compared with the Sun

Sun by a football and put it in the middle of a large field. Mercury will then be a grain of sand at approximately 60 feet from our model Sun; Venus, a pea at 120 feet; the Earth, another pea at 165 feet; Mars, a rice-grain at 250 feet; Jupiter, a golf-ball at 850 feet; Saturn, a table-tennis ball at 1550 feet; Uranus, a grape at 3200 feet, and Neptune another grape at 7400 feet. Pluto will be another sand-grain, but its distance from the Sun varies widely, and at times (as now) it is closer-in than Neptune. The nearest star will be a cricket ball at over 8000 miles, so that if we want to include it in our model we will have to choose a very large field indeed!

Next, let us discuss the ways in which the planets seem to move. Mercury and Venus have their own way of behaving, and show lunar-type phases from new to full. In the diagram below I have shown the

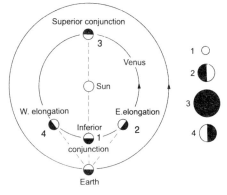

Phases of Venus

orbit of Venus, and I have assumed that the Earth is stationary. In position 1 Venus is at inferior conjunction, i.e. between the Earth and the Sun, so that its dark hemisphere is turned toward us, and normally we cannot see it. If the lining-up is exact, Venus appears in transit as a black disk crossing the Sun's face, but because of the 3.4-degree tilt of Venus' orbit this does not happen often. Transits occur in pairs at an interval of eight years, after which there are no more for over a century; the last pair fell in 1874 and 1882, and the next will be in 2004 and 2012, so that at the present time there can be nobody alive who can remember a transit of Venus (I am looking forward to 8 June 2004). Mercury transits more often; the next occasion will be on 15 November 1999.

Now back to the diagram. As Venus moves along it will begin to show up as a crescent in the morning sky, and by the time it reaches position 2 it will be at greatest elongation, appearing as a half-moon and often rising above the horizon several hours before the Sun. Yet it is further away from us than when it was new, and the apparent diameter is smaller. Oddly enough, Venus is at its brightest when in the crescent stage, and the phase can then be seen easily with binoculars; exceptionally keen-sighted people can make it out with the naked eye.

At position 3 Venus is full, but as it is then to all intents and purposes behind the Sun it is out of view (superior conjunction). The phases are then repeated in the reverse order: gibbous, half (position 4) and then crescent before returning to new. Curiously, the moment of exact half-phase, or dichotomy, does not usually coincide with the time of elongation. When Venus is waxing, dichotomy is a day or two late; when Venus is waning in the evening sky, dichotomy is slightly early. This was first noticed by Johann Schröter in the 1790s, and I once christened it the 'Schröter effect', a term which has come into general use. Of course it does not mean that Venus is out of position, or that there is anything wrong with the calculations; it is due to effects of Venus' dense, cloudy atmosphere. With Mercury, where the maximum elongation from the Sun is never as great as 30 degrees, there is no Schröter effect, because Mercury has practically no atmosphere.

The superior planets, which lie beyond the Earth's orbit in the Solar System, behave differently. The next diagram shows the path of Mars, where the orbital period is 687 Earth days. When the Sun, the Earth and Mars are lined up, Mars is opposite to the Sun in the sky, and is said to be at opposition, so that it is best placed for study. A year later the Earth has completed one circuit, but Mars, moving more slowly in a larger orbit, has not had time to do so, and the next opposition is delayed until the Earth has 'caught Mars up'. The synodic period of Mars is therefore longer than a year; on average it is 780 days, so that there were oppositions in 1993 and 1995, but not in 1994 or 1996. And because the Martian orbit is less circular than ours, not all oppositions are equally close. At times, as in 1988, the distance between the Earth and Mars may be reduced to around 36,000,000 miles; at other oppositions, such as those of 1995 and 1997, the minimum distance is greater than 60,000,000 miles. The next really close opposition will be that of 2003, when for a brief period Mars will outshine even Jupiter.

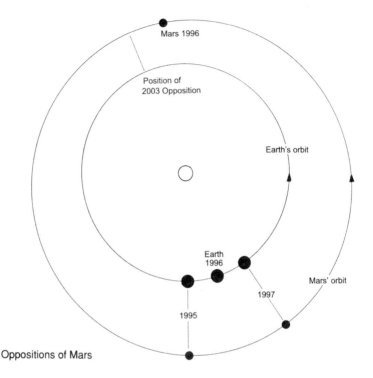

Oppositions of Mars

A superior planet cannot pass through inferior conjunction, but when on the far side of the Sun it does reach superior conjunction.

At right angles to the Sun it is said to be at quadrature. Mars may then show a distinct phase, like that of the Moon a day or two from full, but the phases of the other planets are inappreciable. Moreover, because the outer planets are so far away, the Earth takes less time to 'catch them up', and their synodic periods are shorter; indeed, oppositions of Neptune occur only a couple of days later each year.

A superior planet generally moves from west to east against the stars, but not always, as the next diagram will show; I have again restricted it to Mars, but the principle applies equally to Jupiter and the rest. Some time before opposition, when the Earth is starting to 'pass' Mars, there is a change; Mars reaches a stationary point, and then starts to move in a retrograde or east to west direction against its background. Then there is another stationary point, after which the

Apparent path of Mars in the sky

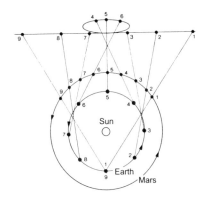

Retrograde motion of Mars

planet resumes its eastward march. In fact, a superior planet seems to describe a long, slow 'loop' against the stars.

All the planets, and all the asteroids, move round the Sun in the same sense as the Earth. This is only to be expected, but, more surprisingly, they do not all rotate in the same sense. Venus is 'upside-down' from our point of view; it spins from east to west, so that if you could stand on the surface of the planet and see the Sun you would find that sunrise would be to the west and sunset to the east (though this is purely academic, since an observer on Venus would be unable to see anything above apart from a cloud-laden sky). Uranus is odd, because its rotational axis is tilted to the perpendicular by more than a right angle, leading to a very peculiar calendar indeed. The reasons for this are unknown. The idea that a planet of this size could be struck by a massive body and literally tipped over does not sound in the least plausible, but when asked to think of anything better I, at least, have to admit defeat. Pluto also has a marked axial tilt, about 122 degrees, but with a very small body of this sort a solution is easier to find.

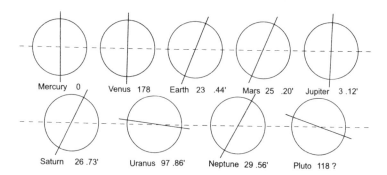

Mercury  0    Venus  178    Earth  23 .44'    Mars  25 .20'    Jupiter  3 .12'

Saturn  26 .73'    Uranus  97 .86'    Neptune  29 .56'    Pluto  118 ?

Axial tilts of the planets

The escape velocity of a planet depends upon its mass; thus Jupiter has an escape velocity of 37 miles per second, while that of Mercury is only 2.6 miles per second, not a great deal higher than that of the Moon. The ability to retain an atmosphere is linked with the escape velocity, because too feeble a pull means that any air will leak away – as has happened in the case of the Moon. It is no shock to find that Mars has a painfully thin atmosphere and Mercury almost none, but what about Pluto, with an escape velocity of less than one mile per second? Pluto does have an atmosphere which is quite extensive, though tenuous. There is, however, an explanation. The speeds at which atoms and molecules move around are very temperature-dependent, and Pluto is so cold that the movements of the atmospheric particles are sluggish enough to be retained. Titan, the largest satellite of Saturn, has an atmosphere which is denser than that of the Earth even though its escape velocity is about the same as that of the Moon; again the very low temperature of Titan is responsible.

There is one other fact which at first sight sounds surprising. The surface gravity of a planet depends not only upon its mass but also upon its diameter, because a body behaves as though all its mass is concentrated at its centre – and the further away you are from the centre, the weaker the pull. This is why Mercury and Mars have the same surface gravity; Mars is the more massive of the two, but it is also larger, so that the surface of the planet is further away from its centre. If you could stand upon Saturn, you would find that you would 'weigh' little more than you do on Earth.

Most of the planets are attended by satellites, but the various families are very unlike each other. Venus and Mercury appear to be solitary travellers in space; any satellites would certainly have been discovered by now. Mars has two tiny moons, Phobos and Deimos, which are more lumps of rocky material and are almost certainly ex-asteroids which wandered too close to Mars and were unable to break free. Jupiter has four large satellites and twelve midgets; Saturn has one major satellite (Titan) and several of medium size, plus some dwarfs; Uranus has five medium-sized satellites and ten which are very small, while Neptune has one major satellite, Triton, and seven which are diminutive. Pluto is a special case, since its companion, Charon, has more than half Pluto's own diameter.

Conventionally, the smaller planets are referred to as 'terrestrial' and the others as 'giants', but we must now modify this, because Pluto cannot be ranked as a proper planet, terrestrial or otherwise. In size it is more or less intermediate between the Moon and the largest asteroid, Ceres. Probably it and Charon must be classed as planetesimals – debris left over, so to speak, when the main planets were formed from the solar nebula. In recent years even smaller bodies have been found in the far reaches of the Solar System, and it is starting to look as though there is a complete gradation from planet-sized bodies through to very small ones.

In Chapter 11 I will have more to say about the less important members of the Solar System, such as asteroids and comets. Meanwhile, it is reassuring to know that the System is a stable place. The Earth's orbit is completely regular, and there is no reason to suppose that there will be any marked change until the far-distant time when the Sun uses up its store of available hydrogen fuel and swells out, with disastrous results. Of course, it is always possible that we will be hit by a wandering comet or asteroid, as Jupiter actually was in July 1994; there must have been major impacts in the past, and there is a popular theory that one strike, some 65,000,000 years ago, caused a change in the world's climate marked enough to eliminate the dinosaurs. However, the chances of any similar event in the near future are very slight indeed.

I am often asked why the Earth, and only the Earth, is suitable for life of our kind. The main reason is that the Earth has the right size and mass, and moves at the right distance form the Sun. As one famous astronomer commented years ago, if conditions were not suitable for us, we would not be here. We would be somewhere else!

# 9

# THE
# INNER PLANETS

It is natural for us to be particularly interested in the planets which move in the inner part of the Solar System, because they are our nearest neighbours and are well within the range of modern rockets. Yet they are not at all like the Earth, and neither are they particularly welcoming. Even Mars, so long regarded as a possible abode of life, is not a place where we could survive under natural conditions.

In any description of the Sun's family it is conventional to begin with Mercury and then work outward. This is logical enough – so let us be conventional.

Mercury is a small world, only 3030 miles in diameter, and since it never comes much within fifty million miles of us it is never glaringly conspicuous; there are many people – even some astronomers! – who

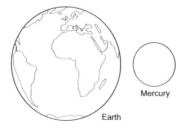

Mercury and Earth compared

have never seen it at all. Actually it can become surprisingly bright, and can outshine any star, but it is never seen against a dark background, and no Earth-based telescope will show much in the way of surface detail. Only one space-craft has been near it: Mariner 10, which made three active passes in 1974 and 1975 before contact was lost. Before that, our knowledge of Mercury was meagre, though it was tacitly assumed that the surface was not too unlike that of the Moon.

Of course the orbit was well known, with its 'year' of 88 Earth-days, but the rotation period was not. For a long time it was believed that the axial rotation period was the same as the orbital period, in which case Mercury would keep the same face turned toward the Sun – just as the Moon always keeps the same face turned Earthward, and for much the same reason. However, Mercury's orbit is appreciably eccentric, and the distance from the Sun ranges between 43,000,000 miles and only 29,000,000 miles, so that the orbital speed varies too, and there would have been important libration effects. There would have been a region of permanent day, an area of eternal night, and a narrow intermediate 'twilight zone', where the Sun would bob up and down-over the horizon. Science fiction writers made great play of the Mercurian twilight zone, but in the 1960s it was found that the true situation was not like this at all. Infra-red techniques proved that the dark side is not nearly so cold as it would be if it never received any sunlight. Radar methods were then called in, and established that the real rotation period is 58.6 days, or two-thirds of a Mercurian year, so that all areas of the surface are in sunlight at some time or other – apart from the floors of some deep craters near the planet's poles, which are never shadow-free.

The first serious attempts at mapping Mercury were made over a century ago, by G. V. Schiaparelli in Italy, but before the flight of Mariner 10 the best chart was due to Eugenios Antoniadi, a Greek-born astronomer based in France, who used the 33-inch refractor at the Meudon Observatory, outside Paris, and produced a map showing bright patches and dark areas. He even gave names to the features he drew – for example Solitudo Hermae Trismegisti, the Wilderness of Hermes the Thrice Greatest. Alas, it was later found that the map bears very little relation to the truth, and an entirely new nomenclature has had to be introduced. This was not Antoniadi's fault; he was a brilliant observer, and he followed the sensible course of observing Mercury during daylight, when it was high above the horizon. His failure was due solely to the fact that the planet is so small and so far

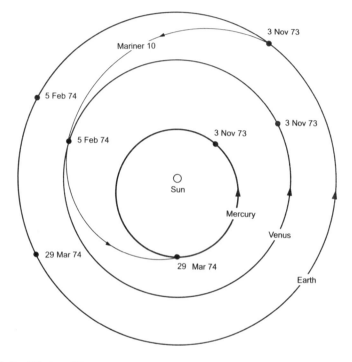

Path of Mariner 10

away that it is an excessively difficult object to see in any detail. Antoniadi was also misled by the fact that whenever Mercury is best placed for observation from Earth, the same side is presented to us.

Mariner 10 was the first probe to make use of the gravity-assist technique. It was launched in November 1973, by-passed Venus in the following February, and made its first rendezvous with Mercury in March 1974. A second encounter took place in September 1974 and a third in March 1975, by which time the on-board equipment was starting to fail, and contact was lost on 24 March. No doubt Mariner 10 is still orbiting the Sun, and still making periodical close approaches to Mercury, but we have no hope of finding it again.

Certainly it performed well, and sent back excellent pictures of mountains, valleys and craters, with one huge ringed formation which has been named the Caloris Basin; there are also scarps and 'intercrater plains' unlike anything found on the Moon. The same regions were seen at each pass, and so we have still been unable to map as much as half of the total surface, but there is no reason to suppose that the remaining areas are any different from those available to Mariner 10.

The most imposing structure is the Caloris Basin, which is over 800 miles in diameter. It has been so named because an observer there would see the Sun directly overhead when Mercury is at perihelion, and the temperature would be around 430° C; in fact Caloris is as hot as any place on Mercury, and even a hard-bitten space-captain would feel somewhat uncomfortable if he chose to land there. On the other hand, the floors of the permanently shadowed craters are intensely cold, and recent radar investigations suggest that they may contain ice, though – as with similar claims for polar craters of the Moon – I admit to being decidedly sceptical.

Mariner confirmed that Mercury is almost airless, and this is not surprising in view of the low escape velocity and high temperature. There is a trace of atmosphere, but it is completely different from ours, and its density is so low – of the order of 1/10,000,000,000 of a millibar – that it corresponds to what we normally call a vacuum. Rather unexpectedly, a magnetic field was found, and it seems that Mercury has a relatively large, heavy core rich in iron; indeed, this core may be larger than the whole globe of the Moon.

It is patently obvious that there can be no life on Mercury. No further probes there have been funded as yet, and the chances of any manned expeditions there in the foreseeable future seem to be nil.

Venus, next in order of distance, is as unlike Mercury as it could possibly be. In size and mass it is almost the equal of the Earth, and its escape velocity is only slightly lower than ours, so that logically it might be expected to have the same kind of atmosphere – but this is emphatically not so. Well before the Space Age it was known that the atmosphere of Venus is so dense and so cloud-laden that it hides the surface permanently. There is no such thing as a sunny day on Venus!

Not many decades ago, Venus was generally termed 'the planet of mystery', even though it is our nearest neighbour apart from the

Moon and occasional comets and asteroids. We did not even know the length of the axial rotation period, and it was suggested that the rotation might be synchronous, i.e. the same as the orbital period of 224.7 Earth days. If so, then there would have been one permanently lit hemisphere and one hemisphere which would be permanently dark; neither would there be marked libration effects, because the orbit of Venus is practically circular.

All that could really be done was to analyse the upper atmosphere, using spectroscopic methods. It was found that the main constituent is carbon dioxide, and since this is a heavy gas which would be expected to sink it was reasonable to assume that carbon dioxide made up most of the atmosphere down to ground level. Since carbon dioxide acts in the manner of a greenhouse, blocking in the Sun's heat, it followed that Venus was likely to be a very torrid sort of world.

Yet opinions differed, and there was also a theory according to which the clouds contained a great deal of $H_2O$. It was even claimed that the surface might be largely ocean-covered, in which case the atmospheric carbon dioxide would have fouled the water and produced seas of soda-water. Another intriguing theory made Venus very similar to the Earth of over two hundred million years ago, when the coal deposits were being laid down; there would be swamps, luxuriant vegetation of the fern and horsetail variety, and primitive life-forms such as giant dragonflies. If so, then Venus might presumably evolve in the same way that the Earth has done.

Little more could be learned from studies of the upper clouds, and the shadings seen from time to time were too vague to give any real clue as to the length of the rotation period – though French observers maintained that the rotation was equal to about four Earth days, in a retrograde or east-to-west direction. The faint luminosity of the night side during the crescent stage, seen by most regular observers of the planet and christened the Ashen Light, was another problem. Few people agreed with the nineteenth-century German astronomer Franz von Paula Gruithuisen that it could be due to illuminations lit by the local inhabitants to celebrate the election of a new Emperor, but nobody could quite explain it.

Then, in 1962, the American probe Mariner 2 by-passed Venus at less than 22,000 miles, and gave us our first reliable information. The surface proved to be very hot indeed; we now know that the maximum temperature is almost 500° C, above even that of Mercury. The atmosphere really is almost pure carbon dioxide, at a ground pressure of roughly 90 times that of the Earth's air at sea-level; there is no detectable magnetic field, and those shining clouds are rich in sulphuric acid. The rotation period is 243 days, longer than Venus' 'year', and is retrograde. Yet the French had been right, too; the upper clouds race round in four days, so that we have a classic case of what is termed super-rotation. All ideas of a pleasant, oceanic Venus had to be abandoned.

The Russians were next in the field, and their automatic landers were able to send back pictures direct from the surface – initially with Venera 7, in December 1970, which survived for almost half an hour before being silenced (earlier Veneras has been literally squashed during their descent through the thick lower atmosphere of the planet). The scene could hardly have been more hostile: a rocky, scorching landscape, about as bright as 'Moscow at noon on a cloudy winter day', to quote the official Soviet source. The rocks are orange, because they reflect the light from the clouds, and there is little wind on the surface, though higher in the atmosphere there must be sulphuric acid rain which evaporates before it can reach the ground.

However, the main information has come from space-craft which have been put into closed orbits round Venus and studied the surface by radar. Magellan, the latest of these probes, was launched in 1989, and continued to send back data until 1994.

Venus is a world of plains, highlands and lowlands; a vast rolling plain covers 60 per cent of the surface, with highlands accounting for only eight per cent. There are two large upland areas, Ishtar Terra in the northern hemisphere and Aphrodite Terra mainly in the south; Aphrodite is about the size of Africa, while the area of Ishtar is much the same as that of Australia. There are also some smaller highland areas, notably Beta Regio, where we find a massive shield volcano – Rhea Mons – which may quite well be erupting at the present time; another probably active area, adjoining Aphrodite, has been nick-named the Scorpion's Tail.

In one way the situation on Venus differs markedly from that on Earth. The terrestrial crust is divided up into various large plates which drift around over the hot mantle, so that a volcano appearing at a 'hot spot' near the boundary of a plate will stay there indefinitely.

Thus one of the main Hawaiian volcanoes, Mauna Kea, has been carried away from the underlying hot spot, and has become extinct; the original site is now occupied by another shield volcano, Mauna Loa, which is very active indeed. On Venus there are no comparable plates, and no systematic movement of the crust, so that when a volcano is born it can stay above its hot spot for a very long time, giving it the chance to become truly enormous.

The radar maps show features of all kinds. Craters abound, some of them very large indeed – well over 150 miles in diameter. There are ridges, valleys, channels and strange volcanic structures which look superficially rather like mushrooms. There are the curious 'arachnoids', circular volcanic features surrounded by complex troughs, and there are circular lowland areas which are characterised by intersecting ridges and grooves. These used to be call 'parquet areas', but the term was regarded as unscientific, and the regions are now known officially as 'tesserae'. The deepest valley, Diana Chasma in the Aphrodite area, goes down for over a mile below the mean radius of the planet, while the highest peaks, the Maxwell Mountains adjoining Ishtar, rise to over six miles.

Clearly the features found on Venus had to be named, and to be Politically Correct it was laid down that all the chosen names must be female. Thus we have Nightingale, Earhart, Helen, Guinevere and others which are equally familiar – but others were less well-known, such as Quetzalpetlatl, Al-Taymuriyya, Erxleben and Xiao Hong. (In case you are wondering, Quetzalpetlatl is an Aztec fertility goddess, Al-Taymurlyya is an Egyptian authoress, Erxleben is a German scholar and Xiao Hong is a Chinese novelist.) The only masculine name honours the great Scottish mathematician James Clerk Maxwell. This particular name had already been given before the official decree was ratified!

Why is Venus so unlike the Earth? The answer can only lie in its lesser distance from the Sun. It seems that in the early days of the Solar System the Sun was less luminous than it is now, in which case Venus and the Earth may have started to evolve along the same lines, but when the Sun became more powerful the whole situation changed. Earth, at 93,000,000 miles, was just out of harm's way, but Venus, at only 67,000,000 miles, was not: the oceans boiled away, the carbonates were driven out of the rocks, and in a relatively short time on the cosmical scale Venus was transformed from a potentially life-

Plate 1  NEPTUNE, showing the Great Dark Spot;
Voyager 2, 1989, from 2,800,000 km

Plate 2 THE MOON, from Apollo 17; the Lunar Rover is shown, with Dr. Harrison Schmitt setting up the ALSEP (Apollo Lunar Surface Experimental Package)

Plate 3 SURFACE OF VENUS, from the Russian space-craft Venera 13 (March 1982). Part of the space-craft is shown

Plate 4  THE HUBBLE SPACE TELESCOPE being deployed from the Shuttle, 25 April 1990

Plate 5  THE MOON,
5 hours before full;
Commander H. R. Hatfield

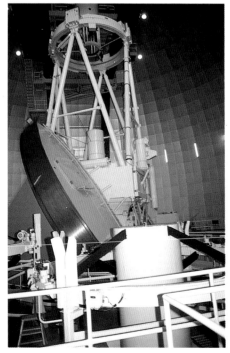

Plate 6  THE ANGLO-
AUSTRALIAN 389 cm
TELESCOPE AT SIDING
SPRING, NSW;
photograph by Patrick Moore

Plate 7  VIKING 1 LANDER ON MARS,
showing the sampler scoop and arm; July 1976

Plate 8  THE GREAT NEBULA IN ORION (M.42);
Palomar Observatory photograph

Plate 9 TRITON, showing the Polar Cap; Voyager 2, 1989

Plate 10 THE PLEIADES STAR CLUSTER; Palomar Observatory photograph

Plate 11 SATURN, photographed with the Hubble Space Telescope, 1990

Plate 12 AX 45 DOMES ON MAUNA KEA: THE UKIRT (foreground) AND THE 88-INCH. Photograph by Patrick Moore, 1990

Plate 13 LAUNCH OF THE ULYSSES SOLAR POLAR PROBE, 6 October 1990, photograph by Patrick Moore bearing world into the inferno of today. Any life which had managed to gain a foothold there was ruthlessly destroyed. It is sobering to reflect that if the Earth had been twenty million miles closer to the Sun, the same thing would have happened here.

No doubt further unmanned probes will survey Venus, and even land there, but certainly there will be no manned expeditions. It has been suggested that we might eventually be able to 'seed' the atmosphere, breaking up the carbon dioxide and sulphuric acid and releasing free oxygen, but this is quite beyond our powers at the moment. In fact, the more we learn about Venus the less inviting it becomes, and it is rather a relief to turn our attention to the red planet Mars.

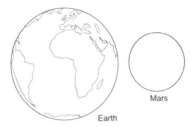

Mars

Earth

Mars and Earth compared

Mars is less unlike the Earth than any other planet. It is much smaller and less massive, and its low escape velocity (just over 3 miles per second) means that it has lost most of any atmosphere it may once have had; what remains is mainly carbon dioxide, but there is not enough of it to produce a Venus-like greenhouse effect, and Mars is a chilly place. At noon on the equator, in summer, a thermometer would rise well above freezing point, but the nights are bitterly cold – far colder than a polar night on Earth – because the tenuous atmosphere is very poor at retaining heat. The surface pressure is below 10 millibars everywhere, which again corresponds to what we usually call a fairly good laboratory vacuum. Certainly there is no chance that future colonists will be able to walk about in the open with only the protection of a warm suit and an oxygen mask.

The axial rotation period is about half an hour longer than ours, so that the 'year' contains 668 Martian days or 'sols'. The tilt of the axis is almost exactly the same as that of the Earth, so that the seasons are of the same general type. There is, however, one important difference. Mars has an orbit which is appreciably eccentric, and the distance from the Sun ranges between over 150,000,000 miles and less than 130,000,000 miles. As with Earth, southern summer occurs at perihelion, so that the southern summers are shorter and hotter than those of the north, while the winters are longer and colder. The effect is very marked, because there is no ocean to stabilise the temperature – and indeed there can be no liquid water on Mars, because the atmospheric pressure is too low; water would promptly evaporate (except just possibly at the very bottoms of the deepest basins).

Telescopes show a red surface, with dark patches and white polar caps. The caps consist of ice, but they are not the same as those of Earth, because each consists of an underlying water-ice cap overlaid by a cap made of solid carbon dioxide. Predictably, the caps wax and wane with the Martian seasons; at their greatest extent they are very large and prominent, while at minimum they virtually disappear. The southern cap shows the greater variations in size, because of the more extreme climate in the southern hemisphere.

The dark areas were once thought to be seas, but it soon became clear that this could not be so. Next, it was assumed that the dark regions were old sea-beds filled with primitive vegetation. Certainly they are permanent, and the most conspicuous of them, the V-shaped marking now known as the Syrtis Major, was recorded by Christiaan Huygens as long ago as 1659. Maps were drawn up during the nineteenth century, and various systems of nomenclature were introduced; at first the names were given, lunar-style, in honour of famous scientists, but in 1877 G. V. Schiaparelli drew a new map and proposed a new system, so that the V-shaped feature seen by Huygens and later christened the Kaiser Sea was renamed Syrtis Major. A small telescope will show it when Mars is well placed – that is to say, a month or two to either side of opposition. At times there are dust-storms which cover the whole planet and hide the surface features, but for most of the time the atmosphere is transparent, though it does contain clouds made up of high-altitude ice crystals.

It was Schiaparelli who made the first detailed drawings of the linear features which he called 'canali', or channels. Inevitably this was translated into English as 'canals', and led to the suggestion that we might be seeing artificial waterways, built by the local inhabitants to form a planet-wide irrigation system. Percival Lowell, founder of the great observatory at Flagstaff in Arizona, was firm in his conviction that Mars was the home of a brilliant civilisation. Alas, we now know that the canals do not exist; they were tricks of the eye, and have no basis of reality. The only planet which has canals on its surface is our own Earth. On the other hand it is quite permissible to describe the ochre areas on Mars as deserts; this is precisely what they are, even though they are not 'sandy', and owe their colour to reddish minerals. Mars is, in fact, a rusty kind of place.

Before the Space Age it was still thought that Mars might be reasonably friendly, with a nitrogen atmosphere thick enough to be useful. It was only with the flight of Mariner 4, in 1965, that our ideas changed. The dark areas turned out to be nothing more than albedo features, where the reddish material had been blown away by winds in the thin atmosphere to reveal the darker surface beneath – and instead of being no more than gently undulating, the surface was seen to be heavily cratered, so that Mars was obviously much more 'lunar' than terrestrial. Later space-craft such as Mariner 9, which entered a closed path around Mars in 1971, showed that there are mountains, canyons, valleys, ridges and also massive volcanoes, one of which, Olympus Mons, towers to three times the height of our Everest, and is crowned by a 50-mile caldera. It had been shown on earlier maps, and known as Nix Olympica, the 'Olympic Snow', but nobody had had any idea of its true nature.

The volcanoes are of special interest. It is generally believed that they are extinct, but we cannot be quite sure, and there is no doubt that there was violent activity in the past. The volcanoes are found in various parts of Mars, but most notably in the area of the so-called Tharsis Bulge, where there is a whole line of giant volcanoes besides which our Hawaiian peaks would seem very puny. There are also some deep basins, one of which, Hellas, measures 1370 miles by 1120 miles. It was once believed to be a snow-covered plateau, because it can sometimes appear so bright that it can easily be mistaken for an extra polar cap.

The Mariner pictures also revealed huge canyon systems, dwarfing our much-vaunted Grand Canyon of Colorado, and there were also features which looked so much like dried-up riverbeds that there seems to be no other explanation. (I remember a comment from a celebrated American astronomer: 'If it looks like a duck, waddles like a duck and quacks like a duck, then maybe it *is* a duck'.) In this case there must have been running water on Mars in the distant past, which means that the atmosphere must then have been much denser than it is today.

Yet how old are the riverbeds? It is usually assumed that they are very ancient, but there seems to be a surprising lack of erosion; we know that there is a great deal of dust in the Martian atmosphere, and dust is highly abrasive. There are two alternative explanations, though neither is officially favoured. At present the tilt of the Martian axis of rotation is almost the same as ours (24 degrees to the perpendicular), but it changes in a cycle of about 100,000 years, and at times the inclination may be as much as 35 degrees or as little as 14 degrees. Suppose that at one stage in the precessional cycle the south pole is turned sunward, and that the ices there evaporate, temporarily thickening the atmosphere and making rainfall possible? Again, can it be that Mars goes through periods of intense vulcanism, so that gases and vapours are sent out in sufficient quantity to increase the atmospheric density? In any case, the dry riverbeds are very much in evidence.

If conditions on Mars were once much more pleasant than they are today, it is possible that life might have started to evolve there, dying out when the climate became unsuitable. If so we might expect to find fossils, albeit of a primitive kind. And the question of life was very much in astronomers' minds when, in 1975, the two Viking probes were launched. Their aim was to make controlled landings and then search for any trace of Martian life, past or present. Each vehicle was made up of two parts: an orbiter, and a lander. The two components crossed space together, and when in Martian orbit they were separated, so that the orbiter could continue circling the planet and also acting as a relay for the lander. The two Vikings were perfect twins, and in the event both worked faultlessly.

It was an ambitious project. If a lander came down on a rock, for example, it would be unable to communicate, but luckily this did not happen. Of course the landing sites had been surveyed as carefully as possible; before touch-down, the orbiter of Viking 1 sent back a picture of a rock with light and shade effects which gave an uncanny resemblance to a human face. (It is only too easy to tell the reactions of the various brands of eccentrics!)

The Vikings came down gently, No. 1 in the 'golden plain' of Chryse and No. 2 in the more northerly plain inappropriately named Utopia.

Material was scooped up from the surface, drawn into the space-craft and analysed, after which the results were transmitted back to Earth. The results showed that there is something decidedly curious about Martian chemistry, but no definite signs of organic activity were found, and the general opinion now is that Mars is sterile at the present time. We can do little more until we can send up an automatic sample-and-return probe, which is a very real possibility within the next few years.

Though Mars is closer than any other planet apart from Venus, it is not too easy to 'observe' in detail, because a small telescope will not show much apart from the polar caps and the main dark areas. However, owners of more powerful instruments can do very useful work in monitoring the changes in the polar caps and, above all, tracking clouds and dust-storms.

Mars has two satellites, both discovered by Asaph Hall in 1877; they were named Phobos and Deimos (Fear and Terror) after two attendants of the mythological war-god. Both are tiny, and irregular in shape; Phobos has a longest diameter of less than 20 miles, Deimos less than 10. Viking and Mariner pictures show that both are darkish and cratered, and indeed the largest crater on Phobos (named Stickney; this was the maiden name of Asaph Hall's wife) has one-quarter the diameter of the satellite itself, so that if it had been formed by a meteorite impact Phobos would have been in grave danger of being shattered into fragments.

Phobos and Deimos are very close to Mars. Indeed, Phobos moves at only about 3600 miles above the planet's surface, and it has an orbital period of 7 hours 39 minutes, so that to a Martian observer it would rise in the west, cross the sky at a breakneck speed and set in the east only 4½ hours later. It would be of little use as a source of illumination at night, and it would frequently be eclipsed by the shadow of Mars; it would transit the Sun over a thousand times per year, taking 19 seconds to cross the disk. Calculations indicate that Phobos is in an unstable orbit. It is spiralling very slowly downward, and may well crash on to the planet in 40,000,000 years' time.

Deimos is further out, and would remain above the Martian horizon for two and a half sols consecutively, but its phases would be none too easy to see with the naked eye, and the total light sent to the planet would be little greater than that which Venus sends to us. Unlike

Phobos, it is in a stable orbit.

There seems little doubt that both Phobos and Deimos are ex-asteroids. There is a rather amusing tale linked with them. In the famous *Gulliver's Travels*, Dean Swift described how the astronomers of the flying island of Laputa had detected two Martian satellites, one of which had an orbital period shorter than the planet's 'day'; inevitably this was seized upon by later eccentrics to claim that Swift knew all about them – even though at the time there was no telescope even remotely powerful enough to show them. In fact, there is a simple explanation. Venus has no moon, the Earth has one, and Jupiter – much further away from the Sun – has four; so how can Mars possibly manage with less than two?

Plans are already being worked for sending the first manned expedition to Mars, and it has been suggested that the date could be as early as 2020. This may be optimistic, but at least we may be confident that Mars will be our first planetary target, and it is quite likely that 'the first man on Mars' has already been born. Travel there now seems much less fantastic than reaching the Moon did at the end of the war.

Meanwhile, Mars is there for our inspection. Look at it through a telescope when you have the chance; you will see the white polar ices, the dark areas and the ochre deserts, and you may also see clouds – though, regrettably, you will see no canals.

# 10
## THE
## OUTER PLANETS

Far beyond Mars, and well beyond the main belt of asteroids, we come to the four giants: Jupiter, Saturn, Uranus and Neptune. They are often discussed together, and in many respects this is logical enough, but the Jupiter/Saturn pair is very different from the Uranus/Neptune pair, and each planet has its own unique characteristics. Of course Jupiter is the senior member, and it has even been said that the Solar System is made up of the Sun, Jupiter, and assorted debris, but the others are not to be despised; even Uranus, the least massive of the four, could balance over fourteen Earths.

Jupiter, so aptly named after the ruler of Olympus, is a real giant by planetary standards, but it is not a 'failed star', as has been suggested. A normal star shines because of nuclear reactions going on deep inside it, as we have already noted in the case of the Sun. To trigger off the hydrogen-into-helium reaction, the temperature must rise to around 10,000,000°C, but Jupiter, vast though it is, has only a little more than one-thousandth the mass of the Sun, and the core temperature cannot be more than 50,000°, while 30,000° is probably a better estimate. This is far too low for nuclear reactions to begin; to rank as a star, the mass of Jupiter would have to be increased by a factor of ten.

Yet Jupiter does send out more energy than it would do if it relied entirely upon what it receives from the Sun. There are two possible explanations for this. The globe could be very slowly shrinking, releasing gravitational energy in the process; the rate of contraction would be far too slow to be measured from Earth. However, it is more likely that Jupiter has simply not had enough time to lose all the heat which it acquired during its formation from the solar nebula, between four and five thousand million years ago. The outer clouds are very cold indeed, at a temperature of around −150°C, so that there is no question of Jupiter sending out enough heat to warm its satellite system.

Look at Jupiter through a telescope – even a small one – and you will see a yellowish, flattened globe crossed by dark streaks which are called cloud belts. There is no mystery about the flattening. Though

Flattening of Jupiter

Jupiter's 'year' is almost twelve times as long as ours, it is a very quick spinner, and a Jovian 'day' is less than ten hours long. As with the Sun, we have differential rotation. The mean equatorial period is 9 hours 50 minutes 30 seconds, while that of the rest of the planet is around five minutes longer, but various discrete features have periods of their own, and drift around in longitude. The equatorial regions bulge out; the diameter as measured through the equator is 89,420 miles, while the polar diameter is a mere 83,100 miles. (*En passant*, the difference between the equatorial and polar diameters of the Earth is only 27 miles, but of course the Earth is a rigid body.)

Obviously we can see only the uppermost clouds of Jupiter, and when we try to investigate the lower layers we have to depend upon theory; it was only in the 1920s that it was finally established that Jupiter is not a midget sun. According to the current models there is a hot core, rich in iron and silicates, surrounded by deep layers of liquid hydrogen. Near the core, the hydrogen is so compressed that it takes

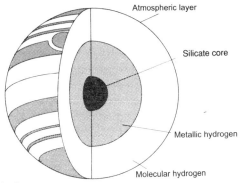

Structure of Jupiter

on the characteristics of a metal, while higher up we come to normal molecular liquid hydrogen. Above this comes the 'atmosphere', at least 600 miles deep, though with a planet such as Jupiter it is not easy to decide just where the 'atmosphere' ends and the main body of the planet begins; the transition must be gradual. It seems that the uppermost clouds are of ammonia ice. Below this comes a layer of ammonium hydrosulphide, a foul-smelling substance made up of ammonia and hydrogen sulphide; deeper still there is a layer of water ice crystals or liquid water droplets, at a pleasantly comfortable temperature. Certainly the main atmosphere consists mainly of hydrogen, which accounts for more than over 80 per cent of the total, and there is spectroscopic evidence of hydrogen compounds such as ammonia and methane. Most of the rest of the Jovian atmosphere is composed of helium.

The famous dark belts dominate the scene. Generally there are several belts prominent enough to be seen with a very small telescope; the diagram given here shows the accepted nomenclature. The North Equatorial Belt (NEB) is always very conspicuous; the South Equatorial Belt (SEB) is much more variable, and has been known to disappear briefly. The region between these two belts has the quickest rotation, and is termed System I, while the rest of the planet is included in System II. As well as the belts and bright zones there are spots, wisps and festoons, most of which show marked changes even over a few rotations of the planet. The most famous feature is the Great Red Spot, which was first recorded during the seventeenth

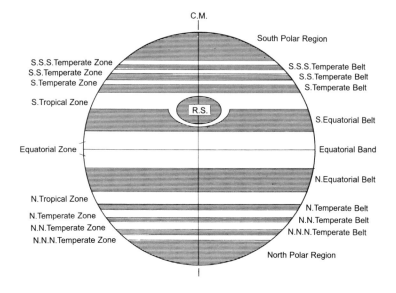

C.M.

South Polar Region

S.S.S.Temperate Zone
S.S.Temperate Zone
S.Temperate Zone

S.Tropical Zone

S.S.S.Temperate Belt
S.S.Temperate Belt
S.Temperate Belt

R.S.

S.Equatorial Belt

Equatorial Zone

Equatorial Band

N.Equatorial Belt

N.Tropical Zone

N.Temperate Zone
N.N.Temperate Zone
N.N.N.Temperate Zone

N.Temperate Belt
N.N.Temperate Belt
N.N.N.Temperate Belt

North Polar Region

Jovian nomenclature

century and has been on view for most of the time ever since; at its greatest extent it is 30,000 miles long by 6,000 miles wide, so that its surface area is greater than that of the Earth. At times it is strongly red, though on occasion it may look grey. Even when at its most obscure its position can usually be found from the Red Spot Hollow, which affects the boundary of the adjacent belt. The Spot drifts along in longitude, but its latitude does not vary much.

Before the space missions nobody knew quite what to make of the Great Red Spot. The idea of a red-hot volcano poking out above the cloud-deck was abandoned long ago, but it was often believed that the Spot was a solid or semi-solid body floating in the atmosphere, vanishing for a while when it sank and was covered up. Thanks to the probes, we now know the Spot to be a whirling storm – a phenomenon of Jovian 'weather', if you like – spinning round anti-clockwise in a period of 11 days, and having a profound effect upon the whole of that part of Jupiter. The colour is still something of a mystery, but phosphorus may be responsible, and certainly there is a rich Jovian chemistry which gives rise to vivid colours not found on any of the other giant planets.

There was a dramatic event in July 1994, when a comet – Shoemaker–Levy 9 – crashed on to Jupiter. The comet is so named because it was the ninth discovery made jointly by two professional astronomers (Eugene and Carolyn Shoemaker) and one amateur (David Levy). Its nucleus had already been disrupted during an earlier encounter with the planet, and had been torn into a chain of over twenty fragments, which impacted in turn between 16 and 22 July. Predictably, the astrologers and the end-of-the-worlders had been in full cry, forecasting doom and destruction; astronomers were doubtful whether anything much would be seen. In fact, the results of the impacts were very obvious, and for a while Jupiter assumed a decidedly unfamiliar appearance, with black patches in the far southern hemisphere showing where the fragments had hit. The storms generated were in many cases much larger than the Earth. The full results will take years to analyse in full, and have already given us new information about the composition of the Jovian clouds. No doubt such impacts have occurred many times in the past, but this is the first time that a cometary suicide has been 'caught in the act' with respect to Jupiter, and it will be strange if we see anything comparable in the near future.

During the 1950s it was found that Jupiter is a source of radio waves, and it was tacitly assumed that there must be a strong magnetic field, but really reliable information had to await the missions of the Pioneers and Voyagers. The Pioneers – Nos. 10 and 11 in the series – were launched in 1972 and 1973 respectively, and each passed by Jupiter after journeys lasting for the best part of two years, though they were very successful they were outshone by the Voyagers, which followed a few years later. It is from the Voyagers that we have drawn most of our detailed information about Jupiter.

Voyager 2 was launched on 20 August 1977, and by-passed Jupiter on 8 July 1979 at a range of 440,000 miles. Voyager 1 began its journey slightly later, on 5 September 1977, but travelled in a more economical path, and made its pass of Jupiter on 5 March 1979 at a minimum distance of only 217,000 miles. This was somewhat risky, because the earlier Pioneers had confirmed that Jupiter is associated with strong zones of radiation – and it is quite definite that any astronaut foolish enough to venture within 100,000 miles of those innocent-looking clouds would die very quickly and very unpleasantly from radiation poisoning. Both Voyagers were programmed to pass as quickly as possible over the equatorial regions of the globe, where the danger is at its worst.

Detailed analyses were made of the clouds, and the favoured model of the interior was confirmed as far as possible. It became patently clear that Jupiter is a world in constant turmoil; storms rage unceasingly, with lightning and, no doubt, thunder. Aurorae were recorded on the night side. Moreover, the Voyagers show that Jupiter has rings, though they are dark and obscure and not in the least like the glorious ring-system of Saturn.

The next impact on Jupiter was man-made. The Galileo probe was launched on 18 October 1989, and after a somewhat circuitous journey reached Jupiter on 7 December 1995. It was made up of two parts: an orbiter, and an entry probe, which were separated well before arrival. The entry probe plunged into the Jovian clouds at over 106,000 m.p.h., and sent back signals for 57 minutes before being destroyed. There were several surprises – mainly the fact that signs of the expected watery layer did not show up. Meanwhile, the orbiting section of Galileo entered a closed path round the planet, and began sending back information not only about Jupiter itself, but about its satellites – which have proved to be even more interesting than had been expected in the pre-Space Age.

Galileo, with his primitive telescope, observed the four main satellites in 1610, which is why they are always known collectively as the Galileans, though in fact Galileo was not the first to see them telescopically; priority seems to go to his contemporary Simon Marius, and it was Marius who named them Io, Europa, Ganymede and Callisto (which may be why these names were not generally used in pre-Space Age days). Any telescope will show them, and so will good binoculars, while really keen-sighted people can see Ganymede at least with the naked eye; it was recorded by a Chinese star-gazer, Gan De, as long ago as 364 BC.

All are planetary in size. Ganymede and Callisto are much larger than our Moon, and Ganymede is actually larger than Mercury, though it is less massive and, like the other Galileans, has no appreciable atmosphere. Io is slightly larger than our Moon, and Europa slightly smaller.

Before the probe missions it was tacitly assumed that the Galileans would be icy, cratered and inert. In the cases of Ganymede and Callisto this turned out to be true enough, but Europa is as smooth as a billiard ball, with strange, shallow cracks which make it a map-maker's nightmare. Just why it is like this remains unclear. There have been suggestions that below its icy surface there may be an ocean of liquid water, with lowly life-forms, but all in all this seems highly improbable, and Europa remains an enigma.

But if Europa puzzles us, Io is dramatic. Here we have a red, sulphury surface, with violently active volcanoes. It has been said that Io looks rather like an Italian pizza; there are extensive lava-flows, and the hot volcanic vents with their calderas filled with black lava erupt at temperatures of around 350°C – which is hundreds of degrees higher than the average for the rest of the surface. Vast amounts of volcanic material are sent out, and it now seems that the lavas may be of molten silicate rock rather than liquid sulphur, as used to be believed. The ejected material is spread all round Io's orbit, and the satellite is connected to Jupiter by a powerful electric current; this is no surprise, since it has long been known that Io's position in orbit has a marked effect upon the radio emissions from Jupiter.

It is strange that Io is so active, while Europa and the other Galileans are so inert. The official theory is that Io's interior is 'flexed' by the gravitational pulls of Jupiter plus the other satellites, so that the temperature is kept high. Certainly the eruptions are going on all the time; both the Voyagers recorded them, and they can now be moni-tored from Earth. The Ionian atmosphere is negligible – conventionally, it cannot be regarded as 'atmosphere' at all – and since Io moves in the thick of Jupiter's radiation zones, it may lay claim to being the most lethal world in the Solar System.

The other twelve satellites are very small. Amalthea, discovered by E. E. Barnard in 1892, was imaged by the Voyagers and found to be reddish and irregular, with a longest diameter of 163 miles; the colour may be due to contamination from Io. There are three more tiny satel-lites moving between the planet and the orbit of Io, and beyond Callisto there are two groups each made up of four members; of these only Himalia (diameter 156 miles) is of appreciable size. The outer four satellites have retrograde motion, and are so far from Jupiter that their orbits are not even approximately circular. No doubt they come from the asteroid belt, and were captured by Jupiter in the remote past.

Jupiter is a rewarding object for the user of a small or moderate-sized telescope. The quick spin means that the spots and other markings are carried relatively rapidly across the disk; the shifts are evident even after a few minutes. Timing the moments when the different features reach the central meridian means that the longitudes can be worked out, and rotation periods derived; the central meridian is easy to locate, because of the flattening of the globe, and estimates can be made to an accuracy of less than a minute. Until fairly recent times it was amateur work which gave us our best data about the rotation periods of the Jovian features, and work of this kind is still very useful indeed.

Next in order of distance from the Sun comes Saturn, arguably the most beautiful object in the entire sky. To the naked eye it looks ordinary enough; it takes the guise of a bright, rather yellowish star, whose 'dull' glare led the ancients to name it after the God of Time (also Jupiter's father, and the previous ruler of Olympus). It takes 29½ years to complete one orbit, and is therefore a slow mover in the sky; once identified, it is easy to find again.

In size and mass, Saturn is second only to Jupiter. Though it is of the same basic nature, there are some important differences, and in particular Saturn's overall density is lower; it is actually less than that of water, so that although the mass is 95 times greater than that of the Earth the surface gravity is less than 1.2 times greater. The surface is gaseous, and hydrogen is (predictably) the main constituent, with most of the rest of the atmosphere being made up of helium. Below the clouds come deep layers of liquid hydrogen, and finally a silicate core not a great deal larger than the Earth. The core temperature may be as high as 15,000°C, but the outer clouds are bitterly cold, at around –180°C. Belts and bright zones are visible with a small telescope, but are less pronounced than those of Jupiter, and there is nothing to match Jupiter's Great Red Spot.

There is a magnetic field, much stronger than that of the Earth though not nearly so powerful as that of Jupiter; and Saturn is a quick spinner, which means that its yellowish globe is very obviously flattened. The axial inclination is almost 27 degrees to the perpendicular, much greater than with Jupiter, and the magnetic and rotational axes are almost coincident.

Occasional outbreaks are seen in the form of white spots. There have been two of special note during the present century, one in 1933 (discovered by a skilful amateur astronomer named W. T. Hay; you may remember him better as Will Hay, the stage and screen comedian), and the other in 1990. Both these became very conspicuous, and lasted for some time. Undoubtedly they were due to material gushing up from below cloud-level.

Three space-craft have so far encountered Saturn. The first of these was Pioneer 11, which had already passed by Jupiter (in 1974) and was sent on to Saturn more or less as an afterthought. It sent back good pictures, but the main results have come from the Voyagers, both of which were amazingly successful. Voyager 1 approached Saturn to within a distance of 78,000 miles on 12 November 1980, and Voyager 2 passed by at a mere 63,000 miles on 25 August 1981. At least the radiation danger was known to be much less than with Jupiter, because Saturn's zones are much weaker.

Excellent views of the globe were obtained, but of course the main glory of Saturn lies with its rings, which are made up of vast numbers of particles of water ice, all spinning round the planet in the manner of moonlets; no solid or liquid ring could possibly exist, since it would

Diagram of Saturn's ring system

promptly be broken up by Saturn's powerful pull. There are two main rings, A and B, separated by a gap known as Cassini's Division in honour of the Italian astronomer who discovered it, from the Paris Observatory, in 1675. (Cassini had his problems at Paris. The French King insisted that the new Observatory should be architecturally attractive rather than functional, so that the sky was largely masked by inconvenient turrets and other structures. Eventually, in desperation, Cassini took his telescopes out into the Observatory grounds, and used them from there!) The outer ring A, shows a narrower division which was first definitely recorded by J. F. Encke in 1837. Between the main rings and the planet there is a much dimmer, semi-transparent ring, known officially as Ring C but more commonly as the Crêpe or Dusky Ring.

Naturally, the rings are circular (or virtually so), but from Earth they appear elliptical, owing to the angle at which we see them. When best displayed, as in the early 1990s, they are magnificent even in a small telescope. The Cassini Division is easy to see, and a 6-inch telescope will bring out the Encke Division as well as the Crêpe Ring. However, when the system is edgewise-on, as in 1995, the rings appear only as a thin line of light, and when the Earth and the Sun are passing through the main plane only giant telescopes will show the rings at all. The system measures 169,000 miles from end to end, but the thickness cannot be more than half a mile.

Voyager results showed that the ring system is much more complex than had been expected. There are in fact many hundreds of minor ringlets and narrow divisions, and there are ringlets even in the Cassini and Encke Divisions; the Encke Division even contains a tiny satellite, now named Pan. The brightest ring, B, shows strange dark radial spokes, presumably elevated away from the main plane by magnetic forces. The Voyagers also detected several faint new rings outside the main system, all of which are virtually impossible to see with Earth-based telescopes.

Saturn has a wealth of satellites. Eighteen are definitely known, and several more have been suspected, but only one – Titan – is large; seven are of what may be termed medium size, while the rest are true midgets. Titan is unique among planetary satellites in having a dense atmosphere, which Voyager 1 found to be made up chiefly of nitrogen together with a good deal of methane. Titan's surface could not be seen directly from either Voyager, and all that could be made out was the top of a layer of orange 'smog'. We are still uncertain about the nature of the surface. There may be ponds of chemical substances such as ethane or methane, but the temperature, around −168°, is too low for any form of Earth-type life to exist there. Interestingly, this temperature is close to the 'triple point' of methane, so that methane could exist there as a solid, a liquid or a gas (just as $H_2O$ can do on Earth, as ice, liquid water or water vapour). It is tempting to picture cliffs of solid methane, lakes of liquid methane, and a methane rain dripping down from the orange clouds in the nitrogen sky! We may know more in 2004, when a space-probe in honour of Christiaan Huygens, the discoverer of Titan in 1655, is scheduled to make a controlled landing there. At least we may be sure that Titan is unlike any other world in the Sun's family.

The seven medium-sized satellites are icy and cratered, as the Voyager pictures showed. Mimas has one huge crater which has a diameter one-third that of the satellite itself; Enceladus shows some smooth, almost crater-free areas, so that there may have been relatively recent upwelling of material from below the surface; Tethys seems to be almost pure ice, while Dione has strange 'wispy' features as well as large craters, and Rhea has a battered surface which looks very ancient indeed. Hyperion is shaped rather like a hamburger, with a longest diameter of 224 miles; its orbital period is over 21 days, but its rotational period is 'chaotic', and is at present about 13 days.

Iapetus is particularly interesting, because it is much brighter when west of Saturn than when to the east of the planet. This is because the axial rotation period is the same as the orbital period (79 days) and its two hemispheres are of unequal reflecting power; one is bright and icy, the other as dark as a blackboard. During western elongations it is always the brighter hemisphere which faces us, and Iapetus can then be seen with a small telescope, but when near eastern elongation it is decidedly elusive. Because the mean density of Iapetus is not much greater than that of water, we may be sure that the globe contains a great deal of ice and that the dark coating is a mere stain – though we do not pretend to know quite what it is, or why only Iapetus has this peculiar characteristic.

Of the small inner satellites, Janus and Epimetheus are of interest because they move in almost identical paths, and there seems no doubt that they are parts of a former larger satellite which broke up; each is very irregular in shape, as the Voyager images showed. Periodically they approach each other and exchange orbits, rather as though playing a game of cosmic musical chairs. The outermost satellite, Phoebe, is more than 8,000,000 miles from Saturn, and has retrograde motion, so that it is presumably asteroidal.

Saturn is always worth observing, partly for its beauty and partly because there is always the chance of finding a new spectacular white spot. It is also convenient, inasmuch as it will usually stand a high magnification well. A 6-inch telescope will show Rhea, Iapetus (when at its best) and Dione and Tethys as well as Titan, which is of course an easy object and has even been glimpsed with good binoculars.

Beyond Saturn move the two outer giants, discovered in near-modern times: Uranus in 1781, by William Herschel, and Neptune in 1846 by Johann Galle and Heinrich D'Arrest, who were searching in a position given by the French mathematician Urbain Le Verrier. The two are near-twins in size and mass. Both are around 31,000 miles in diameter; Neptune is very slightly the smaller, but appreciably the denser and more massive. Both seem to be made up largely of 'ices', with hydrogen-rich gaseous atmosphere which form the surfaces we can see.

In some ways the two are genuinely alike, but in other respects they are very different. In particular Neptune has a powerful internal heat source, while Uranus has not; Neptune's rotational axis is inclined at an angle of less than 30 degrees, while with Uranus the tilt is

Magnetic axis of Uranus

98 degrees – more than a right angle, so that there are times when one or other of the poles is facing the Sun, and the Uranian calendar can only be described as weird. Even the Voyager 2 pictures showed very little detail on Uranus, but Neptune proved to be much more dynamic, with one striking feature, now called the Great Dark Spot, and a beautiful blue surface together with high-altitude clouds made

up of methane crystals. Both have obscure ring systems, made up of dark particles and therefore more like the system of Jupiter than that of Saturn, and both are sources of radio emission, though their magnetic axes are well away from the rotational axes and do not even pass through the centres of the globes.

The satellite systems are different, too. Uranus has fifteen attendants, of which only five were known before the Voyager 2 mission; even Titania, the largest of them, is less than 1000 miles in diameter. All are icy, and Miranda, the smallest of the 'original five', has an extraordinarily varied surface with plains, craters, icy cliffs and large enclosures or 'coronae' which were nicknamed race-tracks! Neptune has one major satellite, Triton, which was well imaged from Voyager 2, and is unique in having pink nitrogen snow at its pole, with active nitrogen geysers squirting out from below the surface. Its diameter is 1681 miles, smaller than the Moon but larger than any of the satellites of Uranus – and, incidentally, larger than Pluto. It has retrograde movement, and seems to be a formerly independent body which was ensnared by Neptune. The other satellites are very small, and only one of them, Nereid, was known before the Voyager 2 pass; it is less than 150 miles across, and has a very eccentric orbit round Neptune, more like that of a comet than a satellite.

Neptune's discovery, in 1846, was the result of mathematical calculations by Le Verrier, who showed that Uranus was being pulled out of position by the action of a more distant and then-unknown planet. Decades later Percival Lowell decided on the same grounds that yet another planet awaited discovery, and in 1930, fourteen years after Lowell's death, the ninth planet – Pluto – was discovered by Clyde Tombaugh at the Lowell Observatory in Arizona, within half a dozen degrees of the position given by Lowell. Yet it is very much of a maverick. Its eccentric orbit can bring it closer to the Sun than Neptune can ever be, and this is the current situation; perihelion was last passed in 1989, and not until 1999 will Pluto's distance from the Sun again become greater than Neptune's. But the main puzzle about Pluto is its small size and mass. Its diameter is only 1444 miles, and it is so lightweight that it could not possibly produce measurable perturbations in the movements of giants such as Uranus and Neptune – and yet it was because of these very effects that it was tracked down. Either Lowell's reasonably correct forecast was sheer luck (which I for one find very hard to believe), or else the real 'Planet X' has yet to be found.

Pluto is not a solitary traveller in space. It has a companion, Charon, which is more than half as large as Pluto itself, and the two are close together (less than 20,000 miles apart); the orbital period of Charon is the same as the rotation period of Pluto, 6 days 9 hours. It seems that the two cannot be of proper planetary status; more probably they are 'planetesimals', made of material left over, so to speak, during the formation of the main Solar System. There is an extensive though rarefied atmosphere, but this may not be permanent. As Pluto moves out toward its next aphelion, in 2113, the temperature will become so low that the atmosphere will condense out on to the surface, and for a major part of its 'year', almost 248 times the length of ours, Pluto may be airless. The surface seems to be coated with a layer of carbon dioxide ice; Charon, which has no detectable atmosphere, has water ice on its surface.

Pluto, at magnitude 14, is within reach of an 8-inch telescope, but appears only as a starlike point. The Hubble Space Telescope has been able to show some dark patches on its surface, but no missions to it have been funded as yet. So far as the amateur observer is concerned, the main attraction is in locating it. Occultations of stars by Pluto are very important, and should be observed whenever possible, because the fading of the star before immersion can provide extra clues about Pluto's atmospheric mantle; but for obvious reasons, occultations do not happen very often.

Periodical searches are made for Planet X, assumed to be moving far beyond the orbit of Pluto, but the task is very difficult, because the planet is bound to be very faint – assuming that it exists at all – and we have no reliable clue as to its position. It may be found one day, but meanwhile Neptune and Pluto mark the boundary of the main Solar System.

# 11
# MINOR MEMBERS
# — OF THE —
# SOLAR SYSTEM

In the early 1770s a German astronomer named Titius drew attention to a curious relationship linking the distances of the planets from the Sun. It was popularised by Johann Elert Bode, Director of the Königsberg Observatory, and – rather unfairly – it is generally known as Bode's Law.

Take the numbers 0, 3, 6, 12, 24, 48, 96 and 192, each of which, apart from the first two, is double its predecessor. Add 4 to each. Taking the Earth's distance from the Sun as 10 units, the remaining figures give the mean distances of the planets with fair accuracy – out as far as Saturn, which was the most remote planet known at that time. Here is the table, to which I have added Uranus, Neptune and Pluto for the sake of completeness:

| Planet | Distance by Bode's Law | Actual distance |
| --- | --- | --- |
| Mercury | 4 | 3.9 |
| Venus | 7 | 7.2 |
| Earth | 10 | 10 |
| Mars | 16 | 15.2 |
| – | 28 | – |
| Jupiter | 52 | 52.0 |
| Saturn | 100 | 95.4 |
| Uranus | 196 | 191.8 |
| Neptune | – | 300.7 |
| Pluto | 388 | 394.6 |

When Uranus was found, in 1781, the Bode distance was in fair accord with the actual distance. Of course the Law fails badly for Neptune, and the Bode distance corresponds more closely with Pluto. All in all it now seems that the relationship is sheer coincidence, belonging more or less to the 'take-away-the-number-you-first-thought-of' status. But this was not apparent in Bode's day, and the missing planet corresponding to the Bode 28 began to assume real significance. It ought to be there, but clearly it would have to be small, as otherwise it would have been found long ago.

In 1800 a team of astronomers assembled at Johann Schröter's observatory at Lilienthal, near Bremen. They called themselves the Celestial Police, and agreed to undertake a systematic hunt for the expected planet, so that each member of the team would be responsible for a particular part of the ecliptic. Ironically, they were forestalled. Before they had time to put the scheme into full working order,

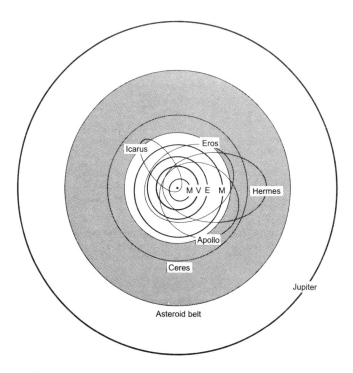

The asteroid belt with some exceptional asteroid orbits

Giuseppe Piazzi at the Palermo Observatory in Sicily chanced upon a slow-moving object which proved to be a small world moving in just the right part of the Solar System. Its Bode distance was 27.7; Piazzi named it Ceres, in honour of the patron goddess of Sicily. However, Ceres was very small, and the 'Police' were not satisfied. Between 1802 and 1808 they discovered three more bodies in the same region: Pallas, Juno and Vesta. No more seemed to be forthcoming, and the Police disbanded in 1815 after Schröter's observatory was sacked by the invading French Army. Then, in 1845, a fifth 'asteroid', Astraea, was found by a German amateur astronomer named Hencke; three more followed in 1847, and since 1848 no year has passed without several new asteroid discoveries. The grand total is now well over 5000, and many more asteroids have been seen without being followed for long enough to have their orbits worked out.

Ceres, with a diameter of 584 miles, is the giant of the swarm, and of the rest only Vesta and Pallas are more than 300 miles across. Only Vesta is ever visible with the naked eye. Most of the asteroids are tiny, and are not regular in shape. Even Pallas is triaxial, though both Ceres and Vesta appear to be more or less spherical.

All asteroids are assigned numbers and names when their orbits have been properly computed. Some of the names are bizarre; the supply of mythological gods and heroes soon ran out, and we now have such oddities as 518 Halawe (named after an Arabian sweetmeat), 1625 The NORC (named after a computer), and 2309 Mr. Spock (honouring a ginger cat which was itself named after the sharp-eared Vulcanian navigator of the fictional starship *Enterprise*). Traditionally, the discoverer of an asteroid is entitled to name it, though the final ratification rests with the International Astronomical Union, and one or two suggested names have been vetoed as being too controversial!

The asteroids have not always been regarded as popular members of the Solar System, since plates taken for quite different reasons were often found to be crawling with unwanted asteroid tracks, and one irritated German went so far as to describe them as 'vermin of the skies'. Yet today they have been rehabilitated, and we regard them as intensely interesting, small though they are. As we have noted, it is now thought that no large planet could form in this region because of the disruptive pull of Jupiter. Moreover, there are well-marked gaps in the main zone where the orbital periods would be exact fractions of that of Jupiter, so that cumulative perturbations keep these gaps swept more or less clean. Asteroids also tend to group in 'families', and collisions must be frequent even today.

We do not yet know much about the surface features of even the senior asteroids, but we do know that there are different types; spectroscopic studies show that some asteroids are rich in silicates, while others are metallic, and Vesta is coated with a layer of igneous rock which was originally molten (The first rough map of Vesta was obtained in November–December 1995 with the Hubble Space Telescope.). Unlike the major planets, they may wander from the ecliptic; the orbital inclination of Pallas, for example, is almost 35 degrees (the orbital period is 4.6 years). Ceres, Pallas and Vesta combined make up 55 per cent of the total mass of the asteroids, but the grand total is a mere 3 per cent of the mass of the Moon, or 0.04 per cent of the mass of the Earth.

Two asteroids have been imaged from close range by the space-craft Galileo, which had to run the gamut of the asteroid zone on its way to rendezvous with Jupiter; it was launched in October 1989, but has had to follow a roundabout route, and – as we have noted – had to follow a roundabout route, and did not rendezvous with Jupiter until December 1995. In November 1991 it passed by Asteroid 951, Gaspra, which turned out to be shaped rather like a distorted potato, with a cratered surface and a maximum diameter of less than 20 miles. Later it imaged Asteroid 243, Ida, which is of the same type, but is slightly larger and is accompanied by a tiny satellite, Dactyl.

Some asteroids depart from the main swarm, and may invade the inner part of the Solar System. The first-discovered of these was 433 Eros, found in 1898, which moves in an orbit crossing that of Mars; at its closest to the Earth it may come within 15,000,000 miles of us, as last happened in 1975. However, this record has long since been broken, and some 'close-approach' asteroids have been known to pass between the Earth and the Moon. One of these, which scraped past us in 1991, has an estimated diameter of only thirty feet, less than half that of a cricket pitch.

It now seems that these wanderers are much commoner than was formerly thought, and several new close-approach asteroids are being discovered yearly. In this case there is always the chance of a collision, and there is some support for the theory that this did happen around 65,000,000 years ago, hurling so much debris into the atmosphere that the Earth's climate was completely changed, with disastrous results for the dinosaurs. Whether this is true or not (and personally

I am distinctly dubious), there is no doubt that we are not immune. If we saw such an asteroid on a collision course it is possible that we might be able to divert it by a nuclear missile, but whether we would have sufficient warning is not clear; for example the 1991 Earth-grazer was discovered only when it had already passed its point of closest approach.

Two asteroids, 1566 Icarus and 3200 Phaethon, spend parts of their orbits closer-in than the path of Mercury, so that at perihelion they must be red-hot. Phaethon moves in the same orbit as the Geminid meteor stream, and may well be its 'parent', in which case we have strong confirmation of the link between comets and small asteroids; this is further supported by the strange case of Asteroid 4015, discovered in 1977, which was subsequently found to have been previously seen in 1949 in the guise of a comet, Wilson–Harrington. I will return to this theme later. Meanwhile, note also that there are a few tiny asteroids whose mean distances from the Sun are less than that of the Earth; such is 2100 Ra-Shalom, which ranges between 43,000,000 and 78,000,000 miles from the Sun in a period of 283 days. It is no more than a couple of miles in diameter, and may be considerably less.

There are also asteroids which keep well outside the main swarm. Such are the Trojans, which move in the same orbit as Jupiter, though they keep prudently either 45 degrees ahead of or 45 degrees behind the Giant Planet and are in no danger of being engulfed (though naturally they oscillate for some way to either side of their mean positions in orbit relative to Jupiter). Some of them are over 100 miles in diameter, though their remoteness from Earth means that they are very faint.

Perhaps the most curious asteroid – if asteroid it be! – is 2060 Chiron, discovered in 1977 by Charles Kowal at Palomar. (Do not confuse Chiron with Charon, the satellite of Pluto. It is a pity that the names are so alike, but they are not associated. In mythology Chiron was a wise centaur who taught Jason and the Argonauts, while Charon was the gloomy ferryman who took departed souls across the River Styx on their way to Pluto's kingdom!) By asteroidal standards it is large – over 150 miles in diameter, perhaps over 200 – and it spends most of its time between the orbits of Saturn and Uranus, which at the time of its discovery was the last place where one would have expected to find an asteroid. It reached perihelion in 1996, when its distance from the Sun was 794,000,000 miles; at aphelion it lies at over

1,700,000,000 miles. The period is 51 years. It caused a major surprise in 1988, when it was seen to be brightening – not spectacularly, but appreciably. It then developed a sort of 'fuzz', as though an icy layer on the surface were starting to evaporate as the temperature rose. This is cometary behaviour, but Chiron is far too big to be a comet, and more likely it is a planetesimal. Calculations show that in 1664 BC it passed within ten million miles of Saturn; this is not much greater than the distance between Saturn and its outer retrograde satellite Phoebe – and Phoebe and Chiron are of almost the same size.

Other exceptional bodies have since been found. Some have very eccentric orbits which take them from the inner Solar System out into the depths; thus 5365 Damocles has an orbit which crosses those of Mars, Jupiter, Saturn and Uranus, while 5145 Pholus moves from within the orbit of Saturn out to well beyond Neptune in a period of 93 years. It is very red, and its diameter may be of from 150 to 200 miles.

In 1992 David Jewitt and Jane Luu, using one of the powerful telescopes atop Mauna Kea in Hawaii, discovered an asteroidal body which was clearly much more remote than Neptune; its mean distance from the Sun is well over 4000 million miles, and its period is 296 years. Other similar bodies have since been found, and it seems that we may be seeing the brightest members of a whole swarm of planetesimals making up the so-called Kuiper Cloud, well beyond the path of Neptune (the name honours the later G. P. Kuiper, who first proposed that such a cloud might exist). It is even starting to look as though there may be a complete gradation from planetesimals through to icy satellites, asteroids and even some varieties of comets. Indeed, short-period comets might well come from the Kuiper Cloud, so before going any further let us say something about these strange, wraithlike objects.

Comets have been described as 'dirty snowballs', and this is by no means a bad description. A brilliant comet, with a long tail stretching across the sky, may appear imposing by any standards, but is not nearly so important as it may seem. The only substantial part of a comet is its nucleus, which is made up of a mixture of ice and 'rubble', and is never more than a few miles across. The average comet travels in a very elliptical orbit, and when far away from the Sun is simply a lump of inert material, but when it draws inward, and the temperature rises, the ices in the nucleus start to evaporate, so that the comet develops a head or coma and perhaps tails. When the comet has passed perihelion, and has drawn back into the cold regions far from the Sun, the head and tails disappear, and the comet reverts to its dormant state.

Tails are of two types: gas (ion) and dust. Both are produced by the effects of the Sun. Light-pressure drives tenuous material outward to produce a straight gas-tail; the solar wind particles also drive material outward to make a curved dust-tail. Both types always point more or

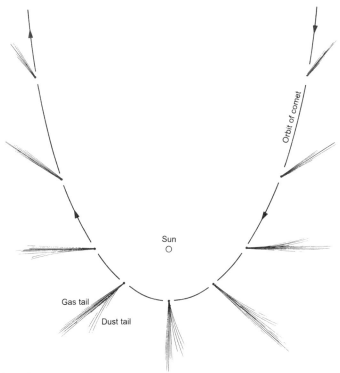

Behaviour of a comet's tail

less away from the Sun, so that when a comet is moving outward after passing through perihelion it travels tail-first. Of course, many small comets never produce tails of either kind, and some of them look like nothing more than slightly 'fuzzy' stars.

It has always been thought that comets come from the so-called Oort

Cloud, a collection of icy objects moving round the Sun at a distance of at least a light-year. (The name honours the Dutch astronomer J. H. Oort, who became the world's leading authority on cometary phenomena.) It was assumed that if a comet were perturbed for any reason, perhaps by a passing star or even by a remote solar planet, it would start to fall inward toward the Sun, and after a journey lasting for many thousands of years would come within our range. One of several things might then happen to it. It might simply swing past the Sun and return to the Oort Cloud, not to return for a very long time indeed. It might encounter a planet (usually Jupiter) and be put into a parabolic orbit, so that it would never return at all; this was the fate of a fairly bright comet (Arend–Roland) seen in the spring of 1957. It might be put into a short-period path with a period of only a few years or a few decades – or it might even fall into the Sun or hit a planet; remember that in July 1994 we witnessed the destruction of a comet, Shoemaker–Levy 9, which committed hara-kiri by impacting Jupiter. Recently it has been suggested that short-period comets come from a much closer Kuiper Cloud, not so very far beyond Neptune and Pluto; this may be so, but in any case we are sure that comets are very primitive bodies, made up of material which was never collected into planets during the formation of the Solar System.

A comet is named after its discoverer or discoverers, or (occasionally) after the mathematician who first computed the orbit. There is also a system according to which a comet is listed by the time of its perihelion passage; this the first comet to pass perihelion in 1994 was 1994 I, the second 1994 II, and so on. No year passes by without several discoveries – some new, and others marking the returns of known periodical comets.

Each time a comet passes through perihelion it loses some of its mass, since material is evaporated to produce the head and tail; this means that by cosmical standards a comet's lifetime is short, and after only a few tens of thousands of years it loses all its volatiles. As we have noted, Comet Wilson–Harrington of 1949 is now purely asteroidal in appearance and has even been given an asteroid number. Short-period comets have to a great extent wasted away, and few of them become bright enough to be seen with the naked eye; several comets which were seen regularly during the nineteenth century have now vanished, and have certainly disintegrated. Such, for the example, were the comets of Brorsen and Westphal, while in 1926 Ensor's Comet faded out when approaching perihelion and was never seen again.

Many short-period comets have their aphelia at about the same distance as the orbit of Jupiter. They are old friends, and we always know when and where to expect them; Encke's Comet, with a period of 3.3 years, has now been seen at over fifty returns, and modern telescopes can follow it all the way round its orbit. It was first seen in 1786 by the French astronomer Pierre Méchain; recovered in 1795 by Caroline Herschel, William Herschel's sister; seen again in 1805 and in 1818, and the orbit was then worked out by J. F. Encke, who predicted that the comet would come back in 1822. It duly did so, and since then it has been seen at every return apart from that of 1944, when it was badly placed in the sky and most astronomers had other things on their minds.

In 1682 Edmond Halley, later to become Britain's second Astronomer Royal, observed a bright comet. He was not the first to see it, but he made careful measurements of it, and came to a remarkable conclusion. Up to that time it had been believed that comets moved in straight lines, passing the Sun only once and then departing, never to return; but Halley realised that the 1682 comet moved in the same way as comets previously seen in 1607 and in 1531. Could they be one and the same? Halley thought so – and he was right. He calculated that if the comet had a period of 76 years it would return once more in 1758. By then Halley was dead, but the comet appeared on schedule, and it was only right that it should be called by Halley's name. Since then it has come back in 1835, 1910 and 1986, though on the last occasion it was badly placed and never became brilliant.

Records show that the returns have been regular, and we can trace the comet back well before the time of Christ. It has not always been popular; when it shone forth in 1066, some months before the Battle of Hastings, the Saxon court regarded it as an evil omen, and in 1456 the then Pope, Calixtus III, preached against it as an agent of the Devil. Certainly comets used to be regarded as unlucky; remember the lines in Shakespeare's *Julius Caesar* – 'When beggars die, there are no comets seen; the heavens themselves blaze forth the death of princes.' The fear was partly superstitious, but partly because of the possibility that a direct hit from a comet would mean the end of the world. Ideas of this sort are not quite dead even yet; at the 1986 return of Halley's Comet several well-meaning organisations loudly proclaimed that the hour of doom was nigh.

In 1986 a whole armada of space-craft was sent to rendezvous with Halley's Comet; there were two Russian probes, two Japanese and one European. The European vehicle, Giotto, was built in Britain, and went right inside the comet's head, sending back close-range pictures of a peanut-shaped nucleus made mainly of ices; it was dark, but with dust-jets issuing from localised areas on the sunlit side. The diameter was no more than 9 miles, and it would take 60,000 million Halley's Comets to equal the mass of the Earth; it loses about 300 million tons of material at each perihelion passage, so that it cannot last indefinitely. It will be back in 2061, though once again it will be badly placed and will not become brilliant (according to the *Anglo-Saxon Chronicle*, it was so bright at the 837 return that it cast strong shadows).

There have been spectacular comets in past years. Chéseaux' Comet of 1744 had at least six tails; the Great Comet of 1811 was visible in broad daylight, as also was the Great Comet of 1843, which incidentally sparked off a major end-of-the-world panic in America. Donati's Comet of 1858 is said to have been the most beautiful on record, with a long, straight gas tail and a scimitar-like dust tail. The 1882 comet cast shadows, and there was also the Daylight Comet of 1910, which appeared a few months before Halley's. The two brightest comets of recent times have been Hyakutake, in 1996, and Hale-Bopp, which became really bright in the spring of 1997 and certainly qualified as a 'great comet'. It remained a naked-eye object for many weeks – but it will not return for some 4,000 years.

Comet-hunting is a favourite amateur pastime, and although it is laborious it is also very rewarding. The procedure is simply to scan the sky with powerful binoculars or a wide-field telescope, noting anything which is unfamiliar. The one essential is an encyclopaedic knowledge of the sky; for example George Alcock, one of the best modern comet-hunters, knows the positions and magnitudes of over 30,000 stars by heart.

There is no doubt at all of the link between comets and meteors, and one celebrated lost comet, Biela's, has provided us with cast-iron evidence. It used to have a period of $6^3/_4$ years, and had been known to reach the third magnitude. When it came back in 1845, it astounded astronomers by breaking in two. The twins returned in 1852, were missed in 1859 because they were so badly placed, and were expected once more in 1866 – but they failed to appear, and have never been seen since. However, in 1872 a shower of meteors was seen to come from the position in the sky where the comet ought to have been, and there is no doubt that these meteors represented the funeral pyre of Biela's Comet.

As we have seen, a meteor is a piece of cometary debris, and when we pass through the 'dusty' trail left by a comet we see a shower of shooting-stars. This happens many times in every year. The meteors of a shower appear to radiate from a definite point in the sky, because they are travelling through space in parallel paths; a good way to demonstrate this is to stand on a bridge overlooking a motorway, and see how the parallel lanes appear to radiate from a point in the distance. Each shower is named after the constellation which contains the radiant. Thus the August meteors come from Perseus, and are known as the Perseids; the November Leonids come from Leo, and so on.

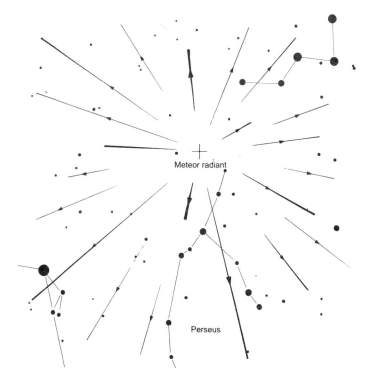

Meteor radiant in Perseus

Not all showers are equally rich. They are classified according to the ZHR or Zenithal Hourly Rate, which is defined as being the number of naked-eye shower meteors which would be expected to be seen by an observer under ideal conditions, with the radiant at the zenith or overhead point. In practice these conditions are never attained, so that the actual ZHR is lower than the theoretical limit. A list of the principal meteor showers is given in the Appendix. (Note that the Quadrantid radiant lies in the constellation of Boötes, the Herdsman; it is the site of an old constellation, Quadrans (the Quadrant) which has been deleted from modern maps.)

The Perseids are the most spectacular of the annual showers, because they have been spread all round the orbit of the parent comet, Swift–Tuttle. Stare up into a clear, dark sky at any time during the first part of August, and you will be unlucky not to see several Perseids. The November Leonids are quite different; they are still 'bunched up', and are rich only when the Earth ploughs through the thickest part of the swarm, as in 1799, 1833, 1866 and 1966. On these occasions it is said that meteors 'rain down from the sky like snowflakes', though unfortunately the 1966 display took place during daylight in Europe, and was seen only from the other side of the world. The parent comet, Tempel–Tuttle, is due back at perihelion in 1999, so that meteor observers will be anxiously awaiting another display of celestial fireworks.

Amateurs carry out valuable work in meteor observing. It is true that radar methods have to some extent taken over, because a meteor trail reflects radar pulses, but visual observations are still useful. The best way to plot the track of a meteor is to hold up a ruler against the path of the shooting-star, so that the beginning and end points can be found with reference to the starry background; again a good knowledge of the sky is needed. Note also the exact time, duration of visibility, brightness, colour (if any) and any other special characteristics. If the same meteor is observed by observers at different sites, it is possible to work out the height by the method of triangulation.

Meteor photography is fascinating; simply point the camera in the appropriate direction, open the shutter and give as long a time exposure as you can without getting dewed up, so that you will 'net' any meteor which happens to flash through the field of view. Of course, not all meteors are members of known showers; there are also sporadic meteors which may appear from any direction at any moment, and all in all it is estimated that 75,000,000 naked-eye meteors enter the Earth's air every 24 hours. Under normal conditions a dedicated observer may expect to see around ten meteors per hour, though during a major shower the number is naturally much higher. And now and then a really magnificent meteor appears; I have seen four which became decidedly brighter than the full moon.

Meteorites are larger bodies, which survive the complete drop to the ground without being burned away. Note that a meteorite is not simply a large meteor, and in fact there is no connection at all. Meteorites come from the asteroid belt, and there is no true distinction between a large meteorite and a small asteroid; it is a question of terminology, though the term 'meteorite' is conventionally limited to objects which have landed on Earth.

Many thousands of meteorites have been collected, and some of these have been observed during their descent. Such was the small meteorite which shot across the English sky on Christmas Eve 1965; it broke up before impact, and distributed fragments round the Leicestershire village of Barwell. There are no reliable reports of any human death by meteorite fall, though it is true that one or two people have had narrow escapes.

Meteorites are of two main types: stones (aerolites) and irons (siderites). They are not always easy to identify, but geologists can recognise them, and if an iron meteorite is cut and then etched with acid it will show characteristic features known as Widmanstätten patterns, not found in terrestrial minerals. Some stony meteorites, known as chondrites, contain small spherical particles (chondrules) made up of fragments of minerals; with other meteorites, chondrules are absent. It has been suggested that some meteorites may have been knocked off the Moon or even Mars, though I admit to being profoundly sceptical.

The largest known meteorite is still lying where it fell, in prehistoric times, near Grootfontein in Southern Africa; to move it would be difficult, because it weight seems to be over 60 tons. The largest meteorite on display is the Ahnighito or 'Tent', which was found in Greenland by the explorer Robert Peary and taken to the Hayden Planetarium in New York, where you can now see it.

Go to Arizona, not far from the town of Winslow, and some way off Highway 99 you will come to a huge crater, the best part of a mile wide, which was certainly made by a meteorite impact over 20,000 years ago. It has become a well-known tourist attraction, and is well worth visiting; the Swedish scientist Svante Arrhenius once described it as 'the most interesting place on earth'. Wolf Creek Crater, in Western Australia, is not so large and is much less accessible, but it is well-formed, and there is no doubt about its origin. Other impact craters are found in the Northern Territory of Australia, Waqar in Arabia, Oesel in Estonia, and here and there in the United States.

There is considerable doubt about the nature of the missile which hit the Tunguska region of Siberia on 30 June 1908. Pine trees were blown flat over a wide area, and the noise was heard hundreds of miles away. It was lucky that nobody lived there; if the object had hit a city, the death-toll would have been colossal. No crater was produced, and it is unclear whether the impactor has to be classed as a meteorite, a tiny asteroid, or a piece of cometary debris. A second Siberian fall occurred on 12 February 1947, in the Vladivostok area, but there is no mystery about this, as over a hundred crater-pits were found and many meteorite fragments collected.

I must also refer briefly to tektites, which are small, glassy objects found in certain restricted areas, such as Australasia and the Ivory Coast. They are aerodynamically shaped, and give every indication of having been heated twice. They were once believed to be meteoritic, but on the whole it now seems more likely that they are of terrestrial origin, and were shot out from volcanoes.

There is a great deal of thinly spread interplanetary material in the Solar System. This is the cause of the Zodiacal Light, a faint, luminous cone seen rising from the horizon soon after sunset or soon before sunrise and extending along the Zodiac – hence its name. It is not easy to see from light-polluted Britain, but from countries with clearer skies it can be very prominent; it is due to sunlight catching particles scattered along the main plane of the Solar System. The Gegenschein or Counterglow, a very dim patch of light exactly opposite to the Sun in the sky, is of similar origin; it is very elusive, and I have seen it only once in my life. So far as I know, it has never been properly photographed.

All in all, the Solar System is a fascinating place, and to us it is of supreme importance. Yet we have to concede that it is a very minor feature of the Galaxy, and it is now time to turn our attention to realms much further afield – far away in the depths of space.

# 12

## —————— THE STARS ——————

No ordinary telescope will show a star as anything other than a point of light; in fact, the smaller a star looks, the better you are seeing it! This is not because the stars are small, but because they are so remote. Measuring their distances is no easy matter, and it defeated the skills even of William Herschel. Success came finally in 1838, due to the careful work carried out by F. W. Bessel in Germany.

Bessel decided to use the method of triangulation. Essentially, this is the same as the method used by a surveyor to work out the distance of some inaccessible object, such as a mountain-top. In the diagram, the observer (O) measures the angle of the mountain as seen from two points, A and B, which are separated by a known distance. The angles BAM and MAB can be found, and hence the angle BMA. Half this angle is known as the parallax. The distance MO can then be found by straightforward mathematics, and this of course is what the surveyor needs.

To measure the distance of a star we require a much longer baseline, and Bessel used the diameter of the Earth's orbit. He selected a dim star, 61 Cygni in the constellation of the Swan, which he had reason to believe must be relatively nearby, and then measured its position against the background of more remote stars, first in January and then in July. During the six-months' interval the Earth moved from one side of its orbit to the other, giving Bessel a baseline of 186,000,000 miles. The parallax shift of 61 Cygni was very small, less than one-third of a second of arc, but it was definite enough, and from it Bessel was able to show that the distance of 61 Cygni is just over

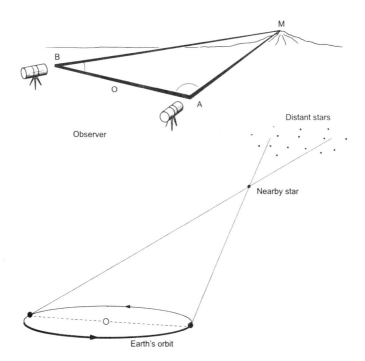

Method of parallax

11 light-years, corresponding to roughly 64 million million miles. Not many stars are as near as that; the closest of all, the dim red dwarf Proxima Centauri in the southern sky, has a parallax of 0.76 of a second of arc, corresponding to 4.25 light-years.

Bessel's reasons for selecting 61 Cygni were twofold. First, the star has a definite proper motion – 4.1 seconds of arc per year; secondly, it was made up of two components separated by almost 30 seconds of arc, so that a small telescope will show them individually. Since both are feeble and red, the fact that they were so far apart gave another indication that they could not be too far from the Sun – at least by cosmical standards.

At the Cape Observatory in South Africa, Thomas Henderson had been making similar measurements of the brilliant Alpha Centauri, one of the two pointers to the Southern Cross, which also has considerable proper motion (in this case 3.6 seconds of arc annually) and is a wide double. Henderson's work was carried out before Bessel's, and was easier, because Alpha Centauri is closer to us – and is only one-tenth of a light-year further away than Proxima, which is a member of the Alpha Centauri group. However, Henderson was in no hurry to publish his results, and failed to do so before Bessel's announcement in 1838.

The parallax method works well out to distances of a few hundreds of light-years, but after that the shifts are swamped by unavoidable errors in observation, so that we have recourse to less direct methods. Most of these involve using spectroscopic analysis to find out how luminous the star really is; we can then compare its apparent magnitude with what is termed its absolute magnitude, and derive the distance. Some stars, known as Cepheid variables, make things easier because they 'give away' their luminosities by the way in which they behave.

Apparent magnitude is a measure of how bright a star looks; the lower the magnitude, the more brilliant the star. Thus magnitude 1 is brighter than 2, 2 brighter than 3, and so on. The most brilliant star in the sky, Sirius, has negative magnitude (–1.5), while the dimmest stars normally visible with the naked eye on a clear night are of magnitude +6. Binoculars can reach down to about magnitude 9, and today electronic equipment used with the world's largest telescopes can penetrate almost to magnitude 30. Conventionally, the twenty-one brightest stars are said to be of the 'first magnitude', ranging from Sirius down to Regulus in Leo, the Lion, whose magnitude is 1.3, but there are 29 more stars between magnitudes 1.5 and 2. The magnitude of the Pole Star is 2.0; the scale is logarithmic, and a star of magnitude 1.0 is exactly a hundred times brighter than a star of magnitude 6.0. A list of the first-magnitude stars is given in Appendix 6.

The apparent magnitude of a star has only a limited connection with its real luminosity, because the stars are at very different distances from us. Consider, for example, Sirius (–1.5) and its nearest rival, Canopus, in the southern sky (–0.7). Sirius looks the brighter by almost a magnitude – but it is only 8.6 light-years away, and no more than 26 times as powerful as the Sun, while Canopus is over 1000 light-years away and could match 200,000 Suns. (The distances of very remote stars such as Canopus are obviously hard to measure accurately, and different authorities give different values. I am here following the official Cambridge catalogue, which seems to be as good as any.) As so often in astronomy, appearances can be deceptive.

The absolute magnitude of a star is the apparent magnitude which it would have if we could see it from a standard distance of 32.6 light-years. From this range Sirius would be of magnitude +1.4, and would just qualify as being of the 'first magnitude', while Canopus would blaze down at magnitude –8.5, and would be the most brilliant object in the sky apart from the Sun and the Moon. The absolute magnitude of the Sun is +4.8, so that it would appear only as a dim naked-eye object.

Why 32.6 light-years? Well, if a star showed a parallax of one second of arc its distance would be 3.26 light-years – a unit known as the parsec. In fact no star apart from the Sun is as close as this, but it explains why we use the standard distance of 32.6 light-years, or 10 parsecs, to determine stellar absolute magnitudes.

The holder of the 'speed record' is Barnard's Star, a dim red dwarf which is only 5.8 light-years away and is the closest of all stars apart from the three members of the Alpha Centauri system, but even here the proper motion is only just over 10 seconds of arc per year, so that it takes 190 years for Barnard's Star to crawl across its background by a distance equal to the apparent diameter of the full moon. This is why the constellation patterns do not change appreciably over periods of many lifetimes. Eventually, of course, they will alter; for example, in the famous Plough pattern of Ursa Major two of the members are moving in a direction opposite to that of the other five, so that if we could come back in (say) 50,000 years the shape would be unrecognisable. But so far as we are concerned, it is fair to say that the constellations are permanent.

Yet a constellation has no real significance, and we are dealing with nothing more than line-of-sight effects. The Chinese and the Egyptians had their own constellation patterns, and if we followed one of their systems our sky-maps would look very different, though the stars would be exactly the same. It so happens that we use the Greek patterns, though with Latin names. Ptolemy, last of the great astronomers of ancient times, listed 48 groups, all of which are still in use though in many cases with altered outlines.

New constellations have been added since Ptolemy's time, notably in the far south of the sky which was inaccessible from Egypt – where Ptolemy is believed to have spent all his life. Moreover, there was a period when astronomers felt bound to add new constellations, stealing stars from accepted groups, so that we have decidedly modern names such as the Telescope (Telescopium) and Antlia (the Air-pump). The eventual sky-map was – and still is – a muddle; Sir John Herschel, son of Sir William, once commented that the constellations seemed to have been designed so as to cause the maximum possible inconvenience. Then, in the 1930s, the International Astronomical Union lost patience and revised the outlines, rejecting some of the most insignificant groups with barbarous names (such as Sceptrum Brandenburgicum and Globus Aerostaticus), and modifying others; the largest of all Ptolemy's constellations, Argo Navis (the Ship Argo) was chopped up into a keel, sails and a poop. Today we recognise 88 constellations, very diverse in size and importance.

In 1603 a German amateur astronomer, Johann Bayer, compiled a new star atlas and introduced the system of allotting Greek letters to the stars. Thus the brightest star in a constellation was lettered Alpha, the second brightest Beta, and so on down to Omega, the last letter of the Greek alphabet. Sirius in Canis Major (the Great Dog) therefore becomes Alpha Canis Majoris. In many cases the letters are out of sequence; for example, in Sagittarius (the Archer) the brightest stars are Epsilon and Sigma, with Alpha and Beta very much 'also rans'. Still, in general the system is a good one, and it has stood the test of time. Years later John Flamsteed, the first Astronomer Royal, gave the stars numbers in order of right ascension, so that for example Sirius is 9 Canis Majoris, and Polaris is both Alpha Ursae Minoris (Alpha of the Little Bear) and 1 Ursae Minoris.

Since the Greek letters will be so often used in the following pages, it may be wise to list them here. They are:

| | | | |
|---|---|---|---|
| α | Alpha | ν | Nu |
| β | Beta | ξ | Xi |
| γ | Gamma | ο | Omicron |
| δ | Delta | π | Pi |
| ε | Epsilon | ρ | Rho |
| ζ | Zeta | σ | Sigma |
| η | Eta | τ | Tau |
| θ | Theta | υ | Upsilon |
| ι | Iota | φ | Phi |
| κ | Kappa | χ | Chi |
| λ | Lambda | ψ | Psi |
| μ | Mu | ω | Omega |

Individual star-names are generally used only for the 21 stars of the first magnitude, plus a few special cases such as the famous double Mizar (Zeta Ursae Majoris) and the red variable Mira (Omicron Ceti). Most of the names are Arabic, and date back for around a thousand years, though a few are older; Sirius is from the Greek word meaning 'scorching', and should be pronounced with a long ī, though most people refer to it as 'Sirrius'. There are cases of stars with several proper names, and there are various spellings and pronunciations; the name of Alpha Orionis, the red supergiant in the Hunter's shoulder, may be spelled Betelgeux, Betelgeuze or Betelgeuse. Nobody has ever been quite sure how to pronounce it; it has even been referred to as 'Beetlejuice'!

The names of fainter stars have fallen into disuse, though they are still met with occasionally. (Incidentally, beware of unscrupulous organisations which claim to be able to name stars upon payment of sums of money. These names are quite meaningless and unofficial, and, to be frank, schemes of this sort can only be described as confidence tricks. Have nothing to do with them.)

Stars are of many kinds. There are doubles, most of which are physically associated or binary systems; there are variables, which change in light over short periods either regularly or erratically; there are giants and dwarfs; there are clusters of stars, some 'loose' and some symmetrical or globular; and there are the huge gas-and-dust patches known as nebulae. And, of course, far beyond our Milky Way system there are the outer galaxies, so remote that in most cases their light takes millions of years to reach us. The stellar sky is full of interest, and so let us now go on a somewhat brief tour. After all, the stars become so much more fascinating when you know which is which.

# 13
## PATTERNS
## OF STARS

Finding your way around the sky is not nearly so difficult as might be thought. There are only a few thousands of stars visible with the naked eye, and the brighter ones stand out at once; when you have identified a constellation you will always be able to recognise it again, because it will not alter (unless a planet moves into it). I well remember that when I set out to learn the patterns, at the advanced age of eight, I made a pious resolve to identify one new constellation every clear night, and after a few weeks I was fairly confident that I could recognise all the main groups.

I am not here setting out to provide a complete guide to the night sky; other books do that. All I hope to provide is some basic information, using the Latin names of the constellations (a full list, with the English equivalents, is given in the Appendix) and adding star magnitudes in brackets. So let us being by observing from the latitude of London, which is approximately 51 degrees north. The method I have always found convenient is to select a few groups which are quite unmistakable, and use them as guides to the rest; much the most useful of these guides are Ursa Major (the Great Bear) and Orion.

## Winter evenings (Northern hemisphere)

This is a good time to commence operations, because both Ursa Major and Orion are on view; Ursa Major stands 'tail down' in the northeast, while Orion is high in the south. Ursa Major never sets over any part of the British Isles, though Orion is out of view for some months during the summer.

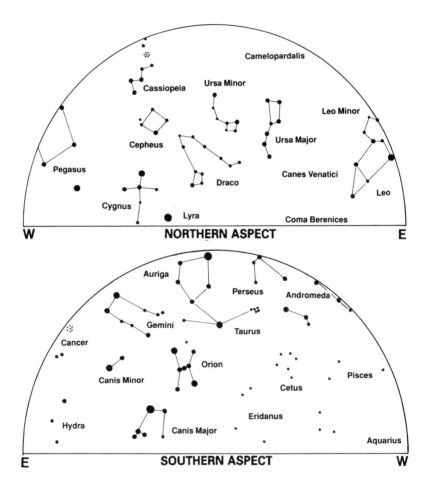

Northern winter sky chart

The seven chief stars of Ursa Major make up the pattern known familiarly as the Plough or, in America, the Big Dipper. All except one are of around the second magnitude, and though they are not outstandingly bright they are very easy to identify, because they lie in an otherwise rather barren area. Look at Zeta or Mizar (2.1), the second star in the Bear's tail, and find the fourth-magnitude companion, Alcor; a telescope will show that Mizar is itself double, with one component decidedly brighter than the other. Between Alcor and the Mizar pair there is a fainter star, which is much more remote from us and simply happens to lie more or less in the same line of sight.

The two end stars of the pattern, Alpha or Dubhe (magnitude 1.8) and Beta or Merak (2.4) are known as the Pointers, because they show the way to Polaris, the Pole Star (2.0) in the Little Bear. Even with the naked eye you can see that Dubhe and Merak are not alike; Dubhe is orange, while Merak is pure white, showing that Dubhe has the lower surface temperature, though it is considerably further away from us and is the more luminous of the two. The other stars of the Plough are Epsilon or Alioth (1.8), Eta or Alkaid (1.9), Zeta, Gamma or Phad (2.4) and Delta or Megrez (3.3). Though it has been given the fourth letter of the Greek alphabet, Megrez is a magnitude fainter than the other members of the Plough. There have been suggestions that it may have faded during the past two thousand years, but this does not seem likely, because it is not the kind of star which would be expected to show secular variation over a period of a few centuries. It is 65 light-years away, and 17 times as luminous as the Sun.

Follow the line of the Pointers, and locate Polaris. Ursa Minor bears a slight resemblance to a dim and distorted Plough, curving down toward Mizar and Alkaid, but it contains only one other fairly bright star, Beta or Kocab (2.1); like Dubhe, Kocab is decidedly orange.

Draco (the Dragon) is a long, sprawling constellation in this part of the sky. It contains no really bright star, but there is one which is worth locating. Almost between Alkaid and Kocab you will find Thuban or Alpha Draconis (3.6). It looks, and is, unremarkable; but it used to be the north pole star at the time when the Pyramids were being built.

If you continue the line of the Pointers beyond Polaris, you will come to Cassiopeia, whose five main stars make up a W or M pattern. The three leaders are of around the second magnitude; Alpha or Shedir is decidedly reddish, and though its magnitude is officially given as 2.2 it is probably slightly variable. Gamma Cassiopeiae, the middle star of the W, is certainly variable; it suffers occasional outbursts, and has been known to rise to magnitude 1.6, though usually it is rather below 2.

More or less between Ursa Minor and Cassiopeia we find Cepheus, notable for the presence of two important variable stars, one of which – Delta Cephei – has given its name to the whole class of short-period variables. I will have more to say about it in Chapter 14.

By late January Leo, the Lion, is coming into view during evenings; by the end of the winter it will be high up after dark. To find it, use the Pointers in the direction away from Polaris; the alignment is not perfect, but it is good enough. In the west the Square of Pegasus, the main autumn constellation, is setting; two of the stars in the W of Cassiopeia can be used to locate it.

Now turn to Orion, high in the south. Here we have an unmistakable pattern, with two brilliant stars, Alpha or Betelgeux (variable, but usually about 0.6) and Beta or Rigel (0.1). The others stars in the main pattern are Gamma or Bellatrix (1.6), Kappa or Saiph (2.1) and the three members of the Hunter's Belt, Epsilon or Alnilam (1.7), Zeta or Alnitak (1.8) and Delta or Mintaka (2.2). All these are hot and bluish-white; Mintaka lies practically on the celestial equator. Rigel – which should logically be lettered Alpha, rather than Beta – is a veritable cosmic searchlight, at least 60,000 times more powerful than the Sun and around 900 light-years away.

Below the Belt you will see a misty patch. This is the Great Nebula, No. 42 in a famous catalogue compiled in 1781 by the French astronomer Charles Messier. It is a stellar birthplace, well over 1000 light-years away, shining because it is being lit up by a multiple star, Theta Orionis, on its Earth-turned side.

Orion's Belt points downward to Sirius in Canis Major, which is much the most brilliant star in the sky (–1.5). It is pure white, but because it is always rather low down as seen from Britain it seems to flash various colours of the rainbow. Star twinkling has nothing directly to do with the stars themselves; it is due entirely to the Earth's unsteady atmosphere, which, so to speak, 'shakes' the light around. The greater the altitude of the star above the horizon, the less it will twinkle. Canis Major is a large constellation with several more bright stars, but it is completely dominated by Sirius.

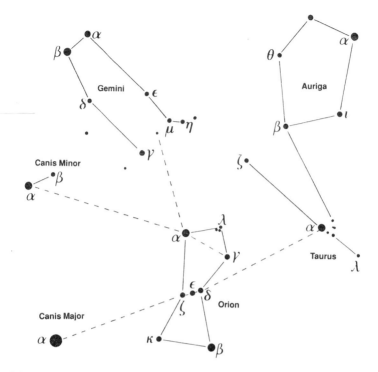

Orion area

Next, use Orion to find Procyon (0.4), Alpha of Canis Minor, the Little Dog. Also in Orion's retinue we find the Twins, Castor and Pollux, in the constellation of Gemini. The two are not true neighbours; Pollux is 36 light-years away from us, Castor 45, and today Castor (1.6) is appreciably fainter than Pollux (1.1). Pollux is orange, while Castor is white – and is, incidentally, a fine binary.

Gemini is crossed by the Milky Way, and is marked by lines of stars extending from Castor and Pollux in the general direction of Betelgeux. Gamma or Alhena (1.9) is prominent, and at the 'foot' of the Twins we find a lovely open star-cluster, M.35.

Upward, the three stars of Orion's Belt show the way to Aldebaran or Alpha Tauri (0.8), the 'Eye of the Bull'. It is not nearly so luminous as Betelgeux, but it is of about the same colour. Extending in a V-formation away from Aldebaran is the open cluster of the Hyades, so spread-out that it is better seen with binoculars than in a telescope. Further away from Orion lies the open cluster of the Pleiades or Seven Sisters, which is without doubt the most celebrated cluster of its type, and is prominent with the naked eye. Taurus itself has no particular shape, but the presence of Aldebaran and the two open clusters makes it unmistakable.

Capella, in Auriga (the Charioteer) is almost overhead during winter evenings; its magnitude is 0.1, and, like the Sun, it is yellowish in colour, though it is far more luminous than the Sun and is actually a very close binary. Auriga is marked by a quadrilateral of stars, one of which, Al Nath, is bright (1.6). Al Nath used to be included in Auriga, as Gamma Aurigae, but for some unknown reason it has been given a free transfer to Taurus, and is now known officially as Beta Tauri. Adjoining Auriga is the rich constellation of Perseus, led by Alpha or Mirphak (1.8). The most famous object here is Beta or Algol, which is normally of the second magnitude, but which fades down to below magnitude 3 every two and a half days – because it is a binary system, and drops in brightness when the fainter component passes in front of the primary and eclipses it.

Between Perseus and the Square of Pegasus we find Andromeda, marked by a line of brightish stars, which is at its best during evenings in autumn. In the south-west lies the rather barren constellation of Cetus (the Whale), and below Andromeda is Aries (the Ram), which is always regarded as the first constellation of the Zodiac even though the vernal equinox has now shifted into Pisces (the Fishes), which is very obscure indeed.

## Spring evenings (*Northern hemisphere*)

By late evenings in April Orion has almost disappeared in the west, though parts of its retinue remain prominent. Ursa Major is almost at the zenith, with Capella in the north-west.

Follow round the 'tail' of the Great Bear (Alioth, Mizar, Alkaid) and you will come to a brilliant orange star, Arcturus. It is slightly above zero magnitude (–0.04), and is the brightest star visible from Britain apart from Sirius. It is the leader of Boötes, the Herdsman, which is well north of the celestial equator even though most of it is not circumpolar from the latitude of London. It has a distinctive pattern resembling a Y, but one of the branches of the Y belongs not

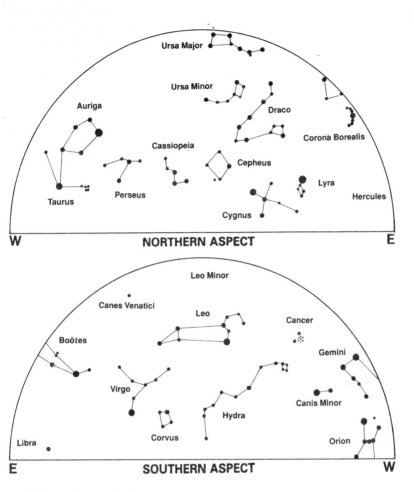

Northern spring sky chart

to Boötes but to the small constellation of Corona Borealis (the Northern Crown), which is one of the few groups to bear some resemblance to the object after which it is named. The little semi-circle of stars is easy to identify, though only one, Alphekka or Alpha Coronae, is of the second magnitude.

Follow the Ursa Major–Arcturus line further, curving it somewhat, and you will come to Spica (1.0) in Virgo, the Virgin. Spica is a white star, more than 2000 times as luminous as the Sun and 250 light-years away; it is actually a very close binary. The rest of Virgo consists of a well-marked Y, covering a large area. The star at the base of the Y, Gamma Virginis or Arich (2.7) is a splendid double with almost equal components. Inside the 'bowl' of Virgo are many faint galaxies, and between Virgo and Ursa Major is Coma Berenices (Berenice's Hair), a loose, extended cluster which looks like a patch of soft radiance in the sky.

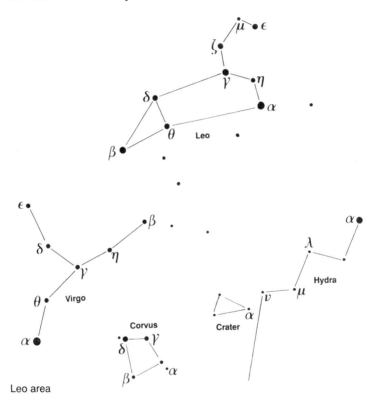

Leo area

As we have seen, Leo (the Lion) can be located by using the Pointers in Ursa Major in the direction away from Polaris. The main part of Leo is marked by the 'Sickle', shaped rather like the mirror image of a question-mark; Regulus (1.3) is the brightest member, while Gamma Leonis or Algieba (2.0) is a fine telescopic binary. Some way from the Sickle is a triangle of stars: Beta or Denebola (2.1), Delta

(2.6) and Theta (3.3). Many of the old astronomers ranked Denebola as being of the first magnitude, equal to Regulus. It is now much fainter, though whether any real change has taken place is doubtful, and more probably we are dealing with mistakes in translation or interpretation.

Next, locate Alphard or Alpha Hydrae (2.0), in the Watersnake. It is clearly reddish, and is known as the 'Solitary One' because there are no other bright stars anywhere near it. The best way to find it is to use the Twins, Castor and Pollux, as pointers. Hydra is the largest constellation in the sky, winding from near Gemini right down to the south of Virgo, but it contains little of immediate interest. Adjoining it are two small constellations, Crater (the Cup) and Corvus (the Crow). Crater is very obscure, but Corvus is conspicuous enough; it lies near Spica, and its four main stars, all between magnitudes 2½ and 3, are easy to identify.

## *Summer evenings* (Northern hemisphere)

Orion has now disappeared; Ursa Major is in the north-west, while Leo and Virgo are low in the west and Pegasus is starting to come into view in the east. Capella is at its lowest, and from the latitude of London it almost grazes the northern horizon, so that any mist or light pollution will hide it.

The scene is dominated by three brilliant stars: Vega (0.0), Altair (0.8) and Deneb (1.2). Years ago, in a television programme, I casually referred to them as the 'Summer Triangle', and the name has come into general use, though it is quite unofficial and does not apply to the southern hemisphere. Vega is in Lyra (the Lyre or Harp), Altair in Aquila (the Eagle) and Deneb in Cygnus (the Swan). Deneb is much the most luminous of the three, and is about 70,000 times as powerful as the Sun; it is so remote that we now see it as it used to be during the time of the Roman occupation. Vega is 26 light-years away, Altair only about 17.

Vega, almost overhead during summer evenings, is of a beautiful blue colour, so that in binoculars it is a splendid sight. Lyra is a small constellation, but contains a surprising number of interesting objects; for example the double-double star Epsilon Lyrae, the eclipsing variable Beta Lyrae, and the most famous of all planetary nebulae, M.57 (the

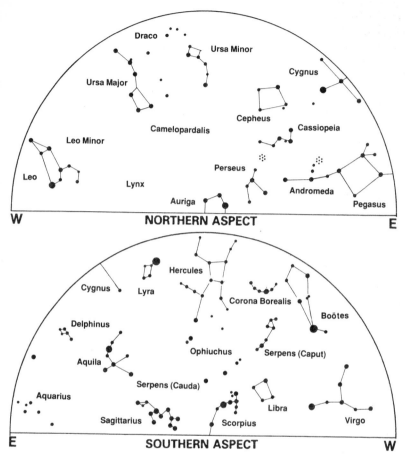

Northern summer sky chart

Ring), which is an easy telescopic object. Like all planetaries it is not a true nebula, but merely a very old star which has blown away its outer layers.

Altair (Alpha Aquilae) is lower down, and is the only member of the Summer Triangle which is not circumpolar from London. It is particularly easy to identify because it is flanked to either side by a fainter star, Gamma (2.7), which is orange, and the white Beta (3.7). Aquila itself is distinctive, with a pattern which really does conjure up the vague impression of a bird in flight. At its southern end the Milky Way is very rich, and here we have the small constellation of Scutum (the Shield), containing the cluster M.16, often nicknamed the Wild Duck.

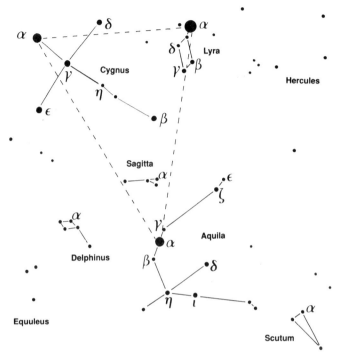

Summer Triangle area

Cygnus is known as the Northern Cross, for obvious reasons. The central star of the X is Gamma (2.2). One member of the pattern, Albireo or Beta Cygni (3.1) is fainter than the rest and further away from the centre, so that it spoils the symmetry, but to make up for this it proves to be a superb coloured double, with a golden-yellow primary and a vivid blue companion. Also in Cygnus there are dark rifts in the Milky Way, due to masses of opaque material blotting out the light of stars beyond. There are several small constellations in the general region, one of which, Delphinus (the Dolphin) looks almost like a very open cluster; newcomers to the night sky have often mistaken it for the Pleiades.

The region enclosed by lines joining Vega, Altair and Arcturus is occupied by three large but dim and ill-formed constellations: Hercules, Ophiuchus (the Serpent-bearer) and Serpens (the Serpent). The only bright star is Rasalhague or Alpha Opriuchi (2.1). Frankly, this is a rather confusing area, and there are not many objects of immediate note other than the globular cluster M.13 in Hercules, which is just visible with the naked eye on a clear night. Rasalgethi or Alpha Herculis, near Rasalhague, is a red variable ranging between magnitudes 3 and 4.

Very low in the south are two magnificent Zodiacal constellations, Scorpius (the Scorpion) – the constellation is often referred to as Scorpio, but Scorpius is the correct name – and Sagittarius (the Archer), parts of which never rise at all over London. Antares (1.0) is the leader of Scorpius; it is fiery red – its name means 'the Rival of Ares' (Mars) – and like Altair it has a fainter star to either side of it. There are many interesting objects in the Scorpion, such as the two naked-eye open clusters M.6 (the Butterfly) and M.7. There is no mistaking the line of bright stars which characterise Scorpius, and Britons always regret that from our latitude it is never really well seen. Sagittarius has no obvious shape, though it is often nicknamed the Teapot; its brightest star easily visible from Britain is Sigma or Nunki (2.0). The Milky Way is exceptionally rich in Sagittarius, and there are glorious 'star clouds' which block our view of that mysterious region, the centre of the Galaxy.

Between Scorpius and Virgo lies the obscure Zodiacal constellation of Libra (the Scales or Balance). Its brightest star, Beta, is said to be the only naked-eye star with a greenish tinge, though most people will certainly call it white. Note that Ophiuchus intrudes into the Zodiac between Scorpius and Sagittarius, so that planets can pass through it even though it is not officially classed as a Zodiacal constellation.

## Autumn evenings (Northern hemisphere)

It is true to say that the evening sky in autumn is less brilliant than at any other time in the year. Scorpius and Sagittarius have disappeared; Orion has not yet come into view, and Ursa Major is at its lowest in the north, though it remains well above the horizon. The Summer Triangle is still on view, now west of the zenith, and Capella is rising in the north-east. Capella and Vega are on opposite sides of

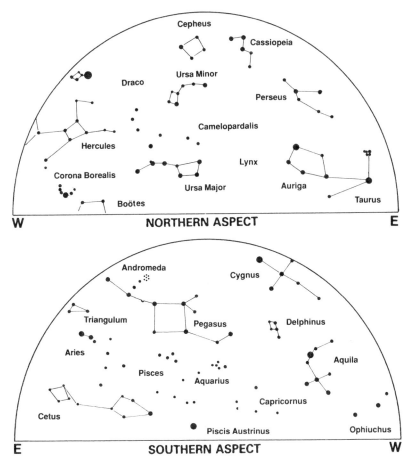

Northern autumn sky chart

the Pole Star, and about the same distance from it, so that when Vega is high up Capella is low down, and vice versa.

The main autumn constellation is Pegasus, named after the mythological flying horse. The four main stars make up a square, which is distinctive enough even though maps tend to make it look smaller and brighter than it really is. The members of the Square are Alpheratz (2.1), Beta Pegasi or Scheat (variable 2.3 to 2.8), Alpha Pegasi (2.5) and Gamma Pegasi (2.8). Alpheratz was once known as

Delta Pegasi, but another dubious transfer has given it to Andromeda, as Alpha Andromedae. The only other bright star in Pegasus is Epsilon (2.4), well to the west of the Square.

Pegasus is not a rich area, and there are not many naked-eye stars inside the Square. Scheat is clearly orange in colour, while the other three members of the Square are white. Andromeda is marked by a

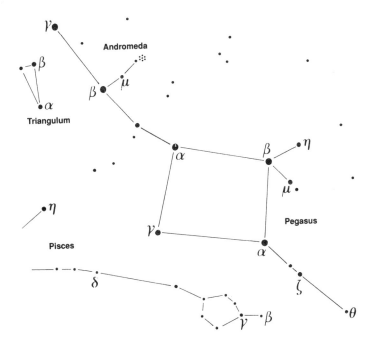

Pegasus area

line of fairly bright stars: the most celebrated object here is the Great Spiral, M 31 on the fringe of naked-eye visibility.

Pegasus can be used to find Fomalhaut in Piscis Australis, the Southern Fish, which is the most southerly of the first-magnitude stars to be visible from Britain. It is a relatively close neighbour, at only 22 light-years; it is white, and 13 times as luminous as the Sun.

Scheat and Alpha Pegasi, in the Square, point downward to

Fomalhaut. Avoid confusion with Diphda or Beta Ceti (2.0), which is roughly indicated by a line passed from Alpheratz through Gamma Pegasi and extended; Diphda is higher-up than Fomalhaut, and almost a magnitude fainter. Cetus (the Whale) is large but dim; its most famous object is Mira, the long-period variable, which has been known to reach magnitude 1.6 at maximum, but which is visible with the naked eye for only a few weeks in every year.

Finally, look for three large, faint Zodiacal constellations. Pisces (the Fishes) consists of a long line of faint stars below Pegasus; Aquarius (the Water-bearer) and Capricornus (the Sea-goat) lie more or less between Pegasus and Fomalhaut. Alpha Capricorni is a naked-eye double. There is little of interest here, but near Beta Aquarii (2.9) we find the magnificent globular cluster M.2, easily visible in binoculars.

This description of the evening sky throughout the year is very incomplete, and many of the smaller constellations have not been mentioned at all, but it should serve as a starting-point, and once you have identified the main groups you will be ready to turn to a more detailed star-map. So let us now turn to the southern hemisphere, and station ourselves at, say, the latitude of Johannesburg (26 degrees south). For most purposes the following notes can be taken to apply to most of South Africa and Australia; some modification is needed for New Zealand – for example Capella never rises over part of South Island, though it can be glimpsed from most of the rest of the country.

One immediately problem is that there is no bright south polar star. The nearest candidate is the obscure Sigma Octantis (5.5), and the whole polar region is depressingly barren. Orion is invaluable when it can be seen, but of course it is out of sight during the winter. Ursa Major is useless. It can attain a respectable altitude from Darwin, and parts of it can be seen over most parts of South Africa and Australia, but it skirts the horizon and is never visible for long; from New Zealand it is to all intents and purposes lost altogether.

The most famous group of the far south is of course Crux Australis, which is actually the smallest constellation in the entire sky, but is crammed with interesting objects. In shape it is more like a kite than a cross, because it lacks any central star, and in any case the symmetry is spoiled by the fact that one member of the pattern is much

fainter than the other three. The main stars are Acrux or Alpha
Crucis (0.8), Beta (1.2), Gamma (1.6) and Delta (2.8). Three of these
are hot and white, but the fourth, Gamma Crucis, is a red giant;
binoculars bring out the colour beautifully. Alpha Crucis is a wide
double, separable with almost any telescope and with a third star in
the field. Note also the lovely cluster round Kappa Crucis, nicknamed
the Jewel Box, and the dark nebula which is known as the Coal Sack.

Crux is almost surrounded by Centaurus (the Centaur), and until
1679 was included in it. The brilliant stars Alpha Centauri (–0.3) and
Beta (0.6) show the way to the Cross, and are known as the Pointers.
Once again appearances are misleading; Alpha Centauri is the nearest

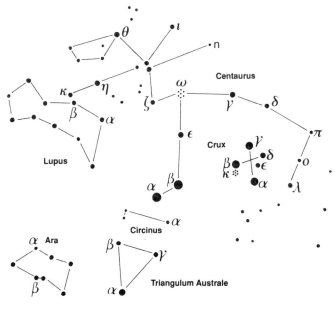

Crux area

bright star beyond the Sun, only a little over 4 light-years away,
while Beta is a real giant, over 10,000 times as luminous as the Sun
and about 450 light-years from us. Although Alpha Centauri is the
brightest star in the sky apart from Sirius and Canopus, it has no
universally accepted proper name. Some air navigators call it Rigel
Kent, and others refer to it as Toliman, but astronomers prefer to call

it simply Alpha Centauri. Like Alpha Crucis, it is a wide, easy double. The nearest star to the Solar System, Proxima, is a member of the same group, but is very faint indeed; whether it is genuinely associated with Alpha is by no means certain. Beta Centauri is often called Agena, but has an alternative proper name, Hadar.

Achernar, in Eridanus (the River) lies on the opposite side of the pole; its magnitude is 0.5, and it is almost 800 times as powerful as the Sun. One of the best ways to locate the polar region is to look directly between Crux and Achernar, but there are no bright stars there, and the whole region appears blank when there is the slightest mist or fog. It contains various small, dim and shapeless constellations with modern-sounding names. In Octans (the Octant) Bayer's system has really broken down; the brightest star in the constellation is Nu (3.8).

## Summer evenings (Southern hemisphere)

At the start of the year Orion is high in the north. From the southern hemisphere, of course, Rigel is in the upper part of the constellation and Betelgeux at the lower right, with the Nebula above the Belt. Sirius is high, and therefore twinkles and flashes much less than it does as seen from Britain. Capella is low over the northern horizon; Crux is rising in the south-east, together with the Pointers.

Canopus (–0.7) is high; it is the leader of Carina, the Keel of the old ship Argo. Carina adjoins Vela (the Sails) and Puppis (the Poop), and the three take up most of the area between Crux and Sirius. The Milky Way is brilliant here, and there are clusters and nebulae as well as bright stars such as Beta Carinae (1.9). There is a very fine open cluster around Theta (2.8), and here too is Eta Carinae, the most erratic variable in the sky, which once outshone even Canopus but is now just below naked-eye visibility. It is associated with nebulosity, and is a fine sight even in a small telescope.

Note also the False Cross, which lies partly in Carina and partly in Vela. It is easily mistaken for the Southern Cross, but is larger, less brilliant and more symmetrical; its members are Epsilon Carinae (1.9), Iota Carinae (2.2), Delta Velorum (2.0) and Kappa Velorum (2.5). Like the real Cross, it has three white members and one – in this case Epsilon Carinae – which is orange.

Note the little constellation of Pictor (the Painter), near Canopus. It

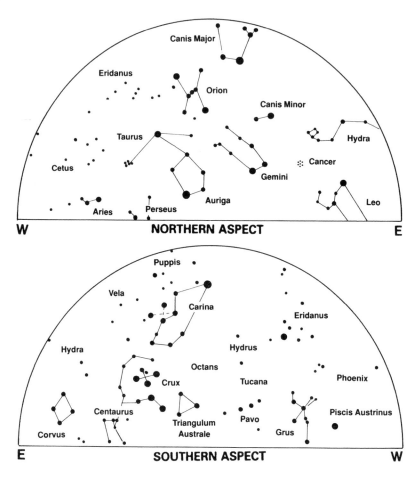

Southern summer sky chart

contains one star of special interest: Beta Pictoris (3.8), which may well be the centre of a planetary system.

Eridanus is a very long constellation, stretching from Achernar in the far south up to Orion, but it contains little of interest apart from the fine, easy double Acamar or Theta Eridani (2.9), the 'Last in the River'. Hydra occupies a large area of the eastern sky, and Leo is coming into view.

# Autumn evenings (*Southern hemisphere*)

Crux and Centaurus are now near the zenith, with Achernar very low down. Canopus and the other stars of the Ship lie to the west; Orion has disappeared by late evening, but Sirius remains. Hydra sprawls across the zenith, with the quadrilateral of Corvus.

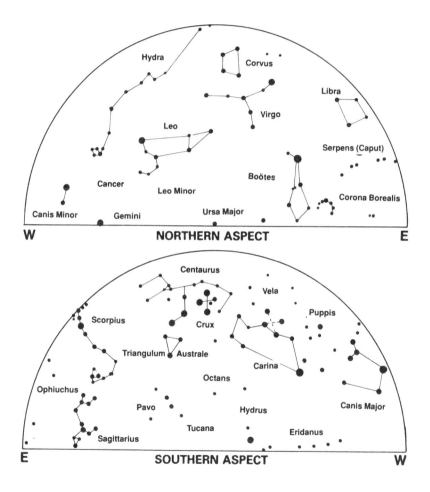

Southern hemisphere autumn

Virgo, Boötes and Leo can be seen in the north. Scorpius is now prominent; it may be said to rival Orion in splendour, and the 'Sting' contains one star, Shaula or Lambda Scorpii (1.6) which is only just below the official first magnitude. Close by it is Lesath or Upsilon Scorpii (2.7). The two give the impression of being a very wide double, but they are not truly connected; Lesath lies in the background, and is four times as remote as Shaula.

## *Winter evenings (Southern hemisphere)*

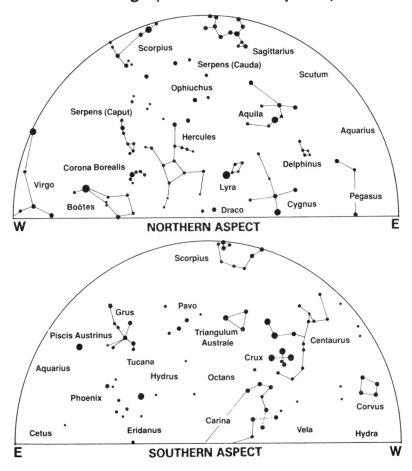

Southern winter sky chart

The scene is dominated by Scorpius, which is almost overhead; here too is Sagittarius, with its glorious star-clouds. This is the best time of the year to see what northerners have come to call the Summer Triangle; Altair is reasonably high up, but Vega and (particularly) Deneb are always very low over the horizon. Arcturus is setting in the west, and much of the northern aspect is occupied by the large, dull groups of Hercules, Ophiuchus and Serpens.

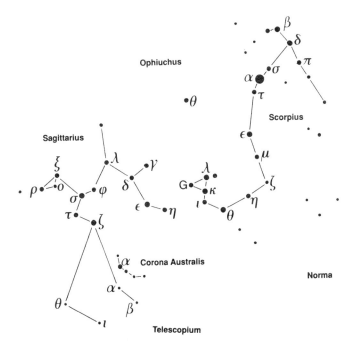

Scorpius-Sagittarius area

Crux is still high in the south-west, with Fomalhaut in the east; Canopus is so low that it will probably not be seen. High in the south we find the four Southern Birds: Grus (the Crane), Pavo (the Peacock), Tucana (the Toucan) and Phoenix (the Phoenix). This is a rather confusing area, and only Grus is at all distinctive, of its two main stars, Alpha (1.7) is white, Beta (2.1) warm orange. The curved line of stars leading away from Alpha is easy to find; two of them, Delta (4.0) and Mu (4.8) look like wide doubles, though in each case we are dealing with line-of-sight effects.

Tucana is redeemed by the presence of most of the Small Cloud of Magellan, together with the globular cluster 47 Tucanae. The cluster appears to be almost silhouetted against the Cloud, but is of course part of our Galaxy, whereas the Cloud is an independent system over 170,000 light-years away. Also high up is the Large Cloud, slightly closer to us and so bright that even strong moonlight will not drown

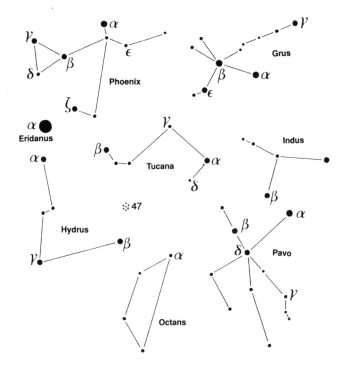

Southern Birds area

it. It contains the great Tarantula Nebula, which is far larger than the Orion Nebula; in fact, if it were within a thousand light-years of us, it would cast shadows. Superficially the Magellanic Clouds look like detached portions of the Milky Way, but to astronomers they are among the most important objects in the sky.

# Spring evenings (*Southern hemisphere*)

By October, Orion is starting to come into view in the east. Crux is very low, which means that Achernar is near the zenith; so too is Fomalhaut, which northern-hemisphere observers will find surprisingly bright. Canopus is rising in the east, with Scorpius and Sagittarius sinking in the west.

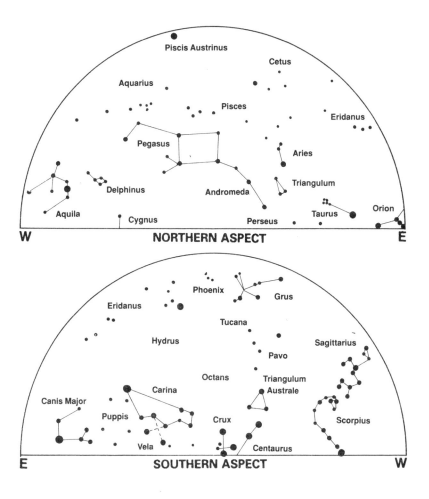

Southern spring sky chart

In the north Pegasus is well on view, and leading away toward the horizon is the line of stars marking Andromeda. Of the 'Triangle', Vega and Deneb have disappeared, though Altair can still be seen low in the west.

I appreciate that this survey of the sky has been watered down to the point of dehydration, but it will suffice for the moment – and once the main patterns have been identified, it does not take too long to learn the rest. Remember, there are only a few thousands of stars visible with the naked eye.

# 14

# DOUBLE AND VARIABLE STARS

Now that we have taken a brief look at the sky as it appears throughout the year, it is time to say more about special types of stars. For example there are stars which are double, or are members of groups; there are stars which change in light and heat output over short periods, and there are some stars which suffer violent explosions, so that they brighten up without warning and remain prominent for a few days, weeks or months before fading back into obscurity.

As we have noted, the most famous of all double stars is Mizar (Zeta Ursae Majoris), in the 'handle' of the Plough – or, if you like, the tail of the Great Bear. It is of the second magnitude, and close beside it is a much fainter star, Alcor (one of the few dim stars to have a generally-used proper name; officially it is 80 Ursae Majoris). Alcor is very easy to see under even average conditions, and it is genuinely associated with Mizar, even though the two are light-years apart; they share a common motion through space, and presumably have a common origin.

Telescopically, Mizar is itself seen to be double; the magnitudes of the components are 2.3 and 4.0, and they are separated by nearly 15 seconds of arc. Both are white, and both are more luminous than the Sun; the primary has 58 times the Sun's power, and the companion could match 12 Suns. They are moving together round their common centre of gravity, but they are at least 40,000 million miles apart, so that the revolution period is tens of thousands of years.

Mizar is a typical binary – that is to say, a physically associated system – but this does not apply to all doubles; we also have optical pairs, where one star is in the background, so to speak, and merely happens to lie more or less in the same line of sight as seen from Earth. Such is Theta Tauri, in the Hyades cluster near Aldebaran. The magnitudes of the components are respectively 3.4 and 3.8, so that they are not very unequal, and are separated by 338 seconds of arc, so that they can be seen separately with the naked eye; the brighter star is white, while the companion is orange. The stars are not bright enough for their colours to be well seen without optical aid, but binoculars show them excellently. In fact the orange star is almost twice as far away as its white companion, and there is no real connection between the two; if we were observing from a different vantage point in the Galaxy, the two Thetas could well be on opposite sides of the sky. It is rather surprising to find that optical doubles are not nearly so common as binaries – and it may even be that single stars such as our Sun are the exception rather than the rule. Stars tend to be gregarious.

Binaries such as Mizar have periods which are so long that the aspect does not change over several lifetimes, but in other cases the changes are obvious even over decades. With Gamma Virginis, in the 'bowl' of the Y of Virgo, the revolution period is only 171.4 years; the components are equal at magnitude 3.5. When I first looked at the pair, during the 1930s, any small telescope would show the components separately, but today they seem much closer together, and by 2010 they will be so close that Gamma Virginis will appear single except with giant telescopes. Of course, this does not mean that the components are genuinely approaching each other; it is simply that we are seeing them at a less favourable angle, and after 2020 the separation will increase once more. With Alpha Centauri, the brighter of the two Pointers to the Southern Cross, the revolution period is a mere 80 years, so that the separation alters quite quickly. This is also true of the position angle (P.A.), which is defined as the angle of the secondary from the primary star, from north (0 degrees) through east (90), south (180), west (270) and back to north. Amateurs can do useful work in measuring the separations and position angles of binary pairs, but very accurate equipment is needed, and the procedure is not nearly so easy as it might sound.

Probably the loveliest double in the sky is Albireo or Beta Cygni, the faintest member of the cross of Cygnus. The primary is golden yellow, the companion vivid blue; the separation is 35 seconds of arc, and in any telescope, or even powerful binoculars, Albireo is a glorious sight. Some red stars are associated with companions which look green by contrast; such are Antares in the Scorpion and Rasalgethi in Hercules. Perfect twins are not uncommon; Gamma Virginis is the classic example, and another is Theta Serpentis, which lies not far from the boundary of Aquila. Each component is of magnitude 4.5, and the separation is over 22 seconds of arc. I always regard Theta Serpentis as one of the most attractive pairs in the sky.

In some cases the components of a binary pair are very unequal. Sirius, for example, has a companion which is very small but amazingly dense; it is a star of the type known as a white dwarf (I will say more about these in Chapter 15). The ratio in luminosity between the two is 10,000 to 1, though the companion is above the ninth magnitude and would be an easy telescope object if it were not so overpowered by its brilliant primary. The revolution period is 50 years. Small though it is, the companion is as massive as the Sun, and it is important to remember that the stars are not nearly so unequal in mass as they are in size and luminosity; the small stars are dense, the large stars rarefied. It is rather like balancing a lead pellet against a meringue.

If the separation between the two components of a binary is very small, no telescope will show the stars individually; but there is another method available, that of spectroscopic analysis. If the two stars are in motion round their common centre of gravity, one component must be approaching us while the other is receding. (Of course this effect must be superimposed upon the overall motion of the pair relative to the Earth, but this can be allowed for.) We can then make use of what is termed the Doppler effect. If a light-source is approaching us, the waves will be 'bunched' up and will be apparently shortened, so that all the spectral lines will be shifted over to the short-wave or blue end of the rainbow background; if the source is receding, the shift will be to the red. Therefore the approaching component of a close binary will have its lines blue-shifted while the receding component will be red-shifted, and all the lines in the spectrum will appear double; if both components are moving in a transverse sense, the lines will be single. Even if only one spectrum can be seen, the binary nature of the system will still betray itself, because the spectral lines of the visible component will oscillate around a mean position.

Both the components of Mizar are spectroscopic binaries (for that matter, so is Alcor), but an even better example is given by Castor, the senior though fainter member of the Twins. Visually, Castor is an easy binary; each component is itself a spectroscopic binary, and there is a third, much fainter member of the group which also turns out to be a spectroscopic binary – so that all in all there are six Castors, four bright and two dim. The view from a planet in such a system would indeed be spectacular.

Multiple stars can also be found. Epsilon Lyrae, close to Vega in the sky, is a naked-eye double, and a small telescope will show that each component is again made up of two, so that we have a double-double or quadruple system. Theta Orionis, in the Hunter's Sword, is nicknamed the Trapezium because of the arrangement of its four main components; and there are various other examples.

We are still unsure about the origin of binary systems. The obvious explanation – the splitting-up of a formerly single star – has been abandoned as mathematically untenable. It may be that in some cases the two components have passed close to each other and have remained linked, but on the whole it seems more likely that the components of both were formed at the same time, and in the same region of space, from the same interstellar cloud.

One particularly important binary is Algol, in Perseus. Normally it shines as a star of the second magnitude, but every two and a half days it begins to fade; it takes five hours to fall to below the third magnitude, remaining at minimum for a mere 20 minutes before taking another five hours to recover its lost lustre. It has long been known as the Demon Star (in the old constellation figure it marks the head of the Gorgon, Medusa whose glance could turn any living creature into stone!), but apparently its odd behaviour was not noticed until the seventeenth century. It was explained in 1783 by John Goodricke, a young astronomer who was deaf and dumb – but who would certainly have achieved great things if he had not died before he was twenty-three.

Algol is not truly variable at all. It is an eclipsing binary, made up of two components, one considerably brighter than the other. When the fainter star passes in front of the brighter, and hides well over 70 per cent of it, Algol seems to give a long, slow 'wink'. There is a slight fading when the primary eclipses the secondary, but the drop in brightness is too small to be noticed with the naked eye. The bright component is 100 times as luminous as the Sun, while the secondary is larger, cooler and less powerful. The distance between the two, centre to centre, is only about 7,000,000 miles, so that no telescope could show them separately even if they were equally bright.

Other Algol variables are known – Lambda Tauri, in the Bull, and the southern Zeta Phoenicis are other naked-eye examples – and there are eclipsing binaries of different type. Sheliak or Beta Lyrae, close to Vega, has components which are much less unequal than those of Algol, and are almost in contact, so that each must be stretched out into the shape of an egg. Variations are always going on, with alternate deep and shallow minima. The full period is almost 13 days, but we also meet with dwarf pairs – named after the prototype, W Ursae Majoris – where the periods are usually less than 24 hours.

At the other end of the scale we have Epsilon Aurigae, one of a triangle of faint stars close to Capella known collectively as the 'Haedi' or Kids. (Capella has been called the She-Goat.) The normal magnitude of Epsilon Aurigae is 2.9, and it has long been known to be a very luminous star, over 200,000 times as powerful as the Sun and at least 4500 light-years away. Every 27 years it fades by a magnitude, so that clearly it is being covered up, but the secondary has never been seen either visually or spectroscopically, and if it did not produce eclipses we would know nothing about it. It is probably a smallish, hot star surrounded by a vast cloud of gas and dust. The latest eclipse began in July 1982 and did not end until June 1984, so that nothing more can be expected yet awhile. Zeta Aurigae, also in the triangle of the Kids, is an eclipsing binary with a period of 972 days, made up of a large red star and a smaller blue star. It has no connection with Epsilon, and it is sheer coincidence that the two lie side by side in our sky; Zeta is little more than 500 light-years away from us.

Of the genuinely variable stars, the most useful to modern astronomers are the Cepheids, which are named after the first-discovered member of the class, Delta Cephei in the far north of the sky – this discovery was, incidentally, made by the remarkable Goodricke. The period is 5.4 days, and the magnitude range is from 3.5 to 4.4. The period and the amplitude are absolutely regular, so that we always know what brightness Delta Cephei will be at any particular moment, and a light-curve can be drawn up by plotting magnitude against time. Cepheids are common enough, and several more are visible with the naked eye – notably Eta Aquilae in the Eagle, Zeta Geminorum in the Twins, and Beta Doradûs in the southern Swordfish.

In 1912 an American astronomer, Henrietta Swan Leavitt, was making careful studies of the two Clouds of Magellan, which lie in the far south of the sky and which look superficially like broken-off parts of the Milky Way. During her work, Miss Leavitt discovered many Cepheid variables, and before long she noticed something very interesting. There was a link between period of variation, and brightness; the longer the period, the brighter the star. Since the Clouds are so far away, it was good enough to say that all the stars in them are at the same distance from us, just as for most purposes we can assume that Charing Cross and Victoria Station are the same distance from New York. It followed that the longer-period stars were actually the more luminous, and eventually it became possible to work out the power of a Cepheid merely by observing it. In fact, Cepheids are 'standard candles', and since they are highly luminous they can be seen over vast distances. They are pulsating stars, swelling and shrinking regularly. The period of pulsation is the time needed for a vibration to travel from the surface of the star through to the centre and back again, which explains why large, powerful stars have longer periods than smaller ones.

Of different type are the Mira variables, named after the first member of the class to be identified, Mira in Cetus (the Whale). It was seen in 1596 by a Dutch amateur, David Fabricius, when it was of the third magnitude. It then disappeared, and was not recorded again until 1603, when Bayer noted it while he was compiling his famous star catalogue. It was again of the third magnitude, and Bayer gave it the Greek letter Omicron. Once more it vanished. Finally, in 1638, another Dutchman – Phocylides Holwarda – realised that it appears and fades away with fair regularity; the period is on average 331 days, and Mira is visible with the naked eye for only a few weeks in every year. At minimum it falls below the tenth magnitude, beyond the range of most binoculars and small telescopes.

Mira variables are very common indeed, though not many attain naked-eye visibility. All are red giants, with periods ranging from a few weeks up to several years; neither the periods nor the amplitudes are constant, and there is no convenient Cepheid-type period-luminosity law. Mira is much the brightest of them, and is usually visible with the naked eye for several weeks in every year. At some maxima it has been known to rise to magnitude 1.6, while at others it becomes no brighter than magnitude 4. Another well-known Mira star is Chi Cygni, in the cross of Cygnus, which has a much longer period (on average 407 days) and a greater range. At its best it has been known to reach magnitude 3.3, but at minimum it sinks to below 14, and since it lies in a very crowded region it is then hard to identify, despite its strong red colour.

Semi-regular variables are related to the Mira stars, and they too are red giants or supergiants, but they have very small amplitudes – seldom more than a couple of magnitudes, usually less – and have very rough periods interspersed with spells of chaotic behaviour. The most celebrated example is Betelgeux, in Orion. On rare occasions (as in late 1993 and early 1994) it can almost match Rigel, while at minimum it is little brighter than Aldebaran. The mean period is said to be 2110 days, but it is very rough indeed. Other conspicuous semi-regular variables are Beta Pegasi, in the Square; Eta Geminorum in the Twins, and Rasalgethi in Hercules.

Some variables are so unpredictable that we never know what they are going to do next. Such is R Coronae, in the 'bowl' of the Northern Crown, which is usually on the fringe of naked-eye visibility, but sometimes fades down to such an extent that a large telescope is needed to show it at all. Apparently it accumulates clouds of soot in its atmosphere, and these clouds cut off the light from below until they disperse. P Cygni, in the Swan, is a highly luminous and unstable star which may throw off shells of material; it has reached the third magnitude, but is generally just above the fifth. A less extreme shell star is Gamma Cassiopeiae, the central star of the W, which is subject to occasional outbursts which take it from below the second magnitude almost to the first. And in the far south of the sky we find the unique Eta Carinae, in the Keel of the Ship. At one time during the last century it outshone every star in the sky apart from Sirius, but for just over a hundred years now it has been below naked-eye visibility. At its peak it shone as brilliantly as six million Suns, in which case it was the most luminous star in the Galaxy, and the total power is much the same even now, though most of it is in the infra-red part of the spectrum. It is associated with nebulosity, and when seen through a telescope looks quite unlike an ordinary star; I have described it as 'an orange blob'.

Novae, still often called 'new stars', are not really new at all, but are dim stars which suffer tremendous outbursts and flare up to many times their normal brilliancy before dying down again. A nova is a binary system, made up of one normal star together with a very old,

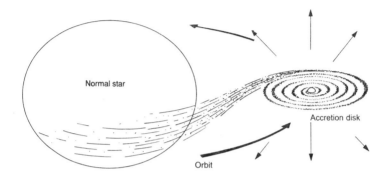

Theory of a nova

very dense companion known as a white dwarf. The white dwarf pulls material away from its primary, and this material builds up until the situation becomes unstable; there is a sudden explosion, and the outburst may take weeks or even years to fade away. Some novae have been really spectacular; thus Nova Aurigae, seen in 1918, reached zero magnitude. Sometimes the outburst dies away quickly, as with the bright star seen in Cygnus in 1975, which flared up to magnitude 1.8 in a few hours but remained a naked-eye object for less than a week; on the other hand Nova Herculis 1934 was prominent for months, though it has now become very faint indeed.

A few stars have been known to suffer more than one nova-like outburst, notably T Coronae in the Northern Crown, which is normally of the tenth magnitude, but which burst forth in 1866 and again in 1946 to reach magnitude 2. And if the build-up of material round the white dwarf becomes really extreme, the whole star may destroy itself in a truly catastrophic outburst. This is termed a type I supernova – but supernovae are very rare, and the last in our Galaxy to become visible with the naked eye was seen as long ago as 1604.

Variable star observation has become one of the most important branches of modern amateur astronomy, because there are so many variables that professional workers cannot possibly monitor them all. The procedure is to compare the variable with nearby stars of known brightness; with practice, eye estimates can be made accurate to a tenth of a magnitude, though specialised instruments known as photo-meters can naturally refine this much further. Searches for novae are also carried out, and here the amateurs have a fine record of discovery. True, work of this kind is time-consuming and laborious, but there is always the chance of finding something new.

# 15
# THE LIFE AND
# TIMES OF A STAR

A careful look into the night sky will show that the stars differ in colour as well as in brightness. True, most of them look white, but a few have a bluish cast, and some are clearly orange or orange-red.

The colours of the stars give a clue as to their surface temperatures; we all know that white heat is hotter than yellow, while yellow is hotter than red. The surface temperature of our yellow Sun is rather below 6000°C; the hottest known stars attain 80,000°, while the coolest of the normal stars shine modestly at temperatures of 2500° or even lower.

The astronomer's chief ally in stellar research is the spectroscope. As we have seen, the Sun – a typical star – yields a spectrum with a rainbow background (due to the relatively high-pressure gas of the photosphere) crossed by dark lines (due to the lower-pressure gases in the chromosphere). Normal stars show spectra of the same basic type, but there are marked differences in detail. For example, very hot stars have spectra dominated by lines of helium and hydrogen, while cool red stars show bands due to molecules of the sort which would be broken up at higher temperatures.

What has been done is to divide the stars into definite spectral types. The modern system was worked out at Harvard Observatory, and was intended to be alphabetical; the hottest stars would be of Type A, followed by B, C, D and so on. Inevitably there were complications, and some classes were found to be unnecessary, while others were out of order. The final sequence was alphabetically chaotic – W, O, B, A, F, G, K, M, R, N, S – but at least it led to the famous mnemonic 'Wow! O Be A Fine Girl Kiss Me Right Now Sweetie' (or, if you prefer, Smack).

Each type is again divided into sub-classes, so that, for example, A5 is half-way between A0 and F0. The main details are given in Table 15.1. Most of the stars are contained in the run from B to M; the first and last types are relatively rare, and R and N are now often combined as Type C.

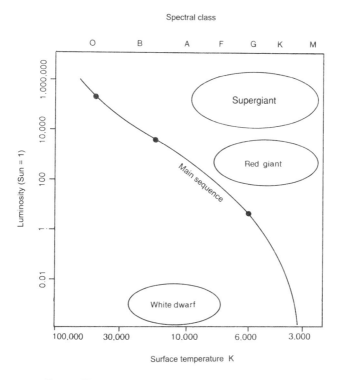

Hertzsprung-Russell Diagram

Shortly before the First World War two astronomers, Ejnar Hertzsprung in Denmark and Henry Norris Russell in America, independently produced diagrams in which the stars were plotted according to their luminosities and their spectral types. It is clear that there is nothing random about the distribution. In a Hertzsprung–Russell or HR Diagram, most of the stars lie on the band known as the Main Sequence, running from the top left to the bottom right. It is also clear that the orange and red stars are divided into two well-marked groups, one very luminous and the other very feeble; this giant and dwarf division is less marked for the yellow stars and does not apply to those which are white (the white dwarfs to the lower left come into a completely different category). Initially it seemed that we might be dealing with an evolutionary sequence. A star would begin by condensing out of the interstellar material, and would at first be large, cool and red, so that it would enter the Diagram from the upper right. As it contracted, under the influence of gravity, it would become hotter and move over to the top left; it would then slide down the Main Sequence, ending up as a dim red dwarf before losing all its energy. Stars of types B and A were said to be of 'early' type; those of type M, 'late'.

It all seemed delightfully straightforward, but it was then found that the whole concept was wrong. The problem is that we cannot (usually) see a star changing its evolutionary state, so that the only course is to pick out which stars are young and which are old. It transpired that far from being stellar infants, the red giants and supergiants such as Betelgeux are cosmical OAPs.

The change in outlook came with the realisation that the stars shine because of nuclear transformations going on inside them, with hydrogen as the main 'fuel'. It then became possible to work out a proper sequence of events, and it emerged that the most important factor is the star's initial mass; massive stars develop much more rapidly than those of lower mass. Moreover, the range in mass is much less than in size or luminosity; there are very few stars more than twenty times as massive as the Sun.

We begin, as before, with the birth of a star from rarefied interstellar material – and we can see the first stages as 'Bok globules' (named in honour of the Dutch astronomer Bart Bok), which are black patches inside nebulae. Orion's Sword contains the great nebula M.42, which is a typical stellar nursery; inside it are many very youthful stars which have not yet become stable, and are varying irregularly. If the mass of the embryo star is less than about one-tenth that of the Sun, the core will never become hot enough to trigger off nuclear reactions,

## TABLE: STELLAR SPECTRA

| Type | Colour | | Surface temperature °C | Examples | Notes |
|------|--------|------|------------------------|----------|-------|
| W | White | | Up to 80,000 | Gamma Velorum (WC7) | Wolf-Rayet stars; bright lines. Expanding shells. |
| O | White | | 40,000-35,000 | Zeta Puppis (O6) | Bright and dark lines. |
| B | Bluish-white | | Over 25,000-12,000 | Rigel (B8) | Helium dominant |
| A | White | | 10,000-8000 | Sirius, Vega | Hydrogen dominant |
| F | Yellowish-white | | 7500-6000 | Procyon, Polaris | Calcium dominant |
| G | Yellow | giants | 5500-4200 | Capella | Metallic lines appear |
| | | dwarfs | 6000-5000 | Sun | |
| K | Orange | giants | 4000-3000 | Arcturus | Strong metallic lines |
| | | dwarfs | 5000-4000 | Tau Ceti | |
| M | Orange-red | giants | 3400 | Betelgeux | Bands due to molecules |
| | | dwarfs | 3000 | Proxima | |
| R | Reddish | | 2600 | No bright example | All very remote |
| N | Red | | 2500 | R Leporis | Strong carbon lines |
| S | Red | | 2600 | Chi Cygni | Almost all are variable |

and the star will simply shine dimly as a red dwarf until it has lost all its energy. With even lower mass, the temperature never rises above a few hundred degrees, so that we are really dealing with a sort of 'missing link' between a star and a planet; bodies of this kind are known, rather misleadingly, as brown dwarfs. A few have been identified with reasonable certainty, but in some ways they remain decidedly enigmatical. It seems that the borderline between a planet and a brown dwarf is about ten times the mass of Jupiter, the senior member of the Sun's family.

If the mass is more than one-tenth that of the Sun, the body attains true stellar rank. It begins to shine; as it shrinks the surface temperature remains the same, and the original cocoon of dust around the star's body is blown away. Irregular flickering continues, and there is a strong stellar 'wind'; this is the so-called T Tauri stage. Condensing to the Main Sequence takes millions of years, but at last the core temperature reaches the critical value of 10,000,000 degrees, and nuclear reactions start. The point on the Main Sequence where the star joins again depends on the mass; the greater the mass, the closer the point of junction to the upper left of the diagram.

The hydrogen-into-helium conversion is adequate to maintain the flow of radiation for a very long time, but it cannot last for ever, and eventually it starts to run low; the core is now composed chiefly of helium. When the hydrogen supply fails, the star shrinks and the core heats up, so that helium can start to react and build up carbon; the star leaves the Main Sequence, and moves toward the giant branch at the upper right of the diagram. After a somewhat complex series of reactions it becomes a red giant, and the results so far as the Earth are concerned will be dire; for a while the Sun will radiate at least a hundred times as powerfully as it does now, and the outer layers will swell out until they engulf the orbits of the inner planets – Mercury and Venus certainly, and very probably the Earth as well. This means that life here cannot hope to survive, and indeed the Sun will have become uncomfortably hot even before then; recent calculations indicate that conditions on our world will become intolerable in little over a thousand million years hence. (Please do not worry. After all, it might be worse – say a mere five hundred million years!) A star in this stage of evolution has become unstable, and is variable in output.

Next, the outer layers are blown away completely, and we have what is inappropriately termed a planetary nebula. The outer layers dissipate in space, and all that is left of the star is its core, which is now only a few tens of thousands of miles across, and is super-dense. The star has turned into a white dwarf, and has moved over to the lower left of the HR Diagram.

The reason for this great density – sometimes over a million times that of water – is that the atoms in the star are crushed and broken. Under normal circumstances an atom is mainly empty space, but in the 'degenerate' matter of a white dwarf there is virtually no waste space at all, and the various components are packed tightly together. The best-known white dwarf is the faint companion of Sirius (often nicknamed the Pup, since Sirius is the Dog-star). The companion has only 1/10,000 the luminosity of its brilliant primary, but it is as massive as the Sun, and a cupful of its material would weigh hundreds of tons.

A white dwarf has been aptly described as a bankrupt star; it has no reserves of energy left, and shines feebly only because it is still shrinking. In the end all its light and heat will leave it, and it will become a cold, dead black dwarf. Obviously we will then be unable to see it, because it will radiate no energy at all, but in any case it is by no means certain that the universe is yet old enough for any black dwarfs to have been produced. The universe, in its present form, seems to be no more than 20,000 million years old at most, and the decline from a white to a black dwarf may take longer than that.

Now consider a star which is more massive still – say over 1.4 times as massive as the Sun. The birth process is the same as before, but everything happens at an accelerated rate, so that the star spends much less time on the Main Sequence before starting to run out of hydrogen fuel; it has of course joined the Main Sequence at the upper left. After the helium has reacted to form carbon, it is the turn of the carbon to start manufacturing heavier elements, and at one stage the star's structure is not unlike that of an onion, with different types of reactions going on at different levels. Iron is produced, and the core reaches the unbelievable temperature of around 3000 million degrees.

It is when the core has been converted into iron that the real crisis begins, because iron will not react in the same manner as the lighter elements. Abruptly, all energy production stops. In a matter of seconds the core collapses; the outer layers fall on to it, and there is a tremendous rebound, so that a shock-wave spreads through the star's body and most of the material is hurled away into space in what is termed a Type II supernova outburst. The luminosity may reach at least five thousand million times that of the Sun, and as the explosion dies down we are left with a cloud of material expanding into space; this material is enriched with the heavy elements which have been created during the build-up to the outburst, and it is out of this enriched material that new stars are formed.

But what of the core of the dying star itself? Even the component parts of the atoms are forced together; protons and electrons combine, and the positive charges of the protons cancel out the negative charges of the electrons, so that the result is a star made up of neutrons.

A neutron star is indeed bizarre. It is only a few miles across, but the density may be a thousand million times that of water, so that a pin's head of neutron star material would weigh as much as an ocean liner. According to theory, the outer surface of a neutron star is crystalline and iron-rich; below comes neutron-rich liquid material, which in turn overlays a core made up of particles about which we know almost nothing. There is a powerful magnetic field, and the neutron star is spinning round rapidly, perhaps many times per second. This tiny object is all that is left of the formerly very massive star.

In 1967 Jocelyn Bell Burnell, a radio astronomer at Cambridge University, made an unexpected discovery. She found a radio source which seemed to be 'ticking' so regularly and so rapidly that at first it was thought that the transmissions might be artificial. The 'LGM' or Little Green Men theory was soon discounted, but the pulsating source remained a mystery for some time. Finally, the cause was found. A 'pulsar' is a rapidly spinning neutron star; the magnetic axis is inclined to the axis of rotation, and beams of radiation are pouring out from the magnetic poles, so that every time a beam sweeps across the Earth we receive a pulse. The situation is rather like that of a watcher on the coast being regularly illuminated by the beam of a rotating lighthouse far out to sea.

Hundreds of pulsars have now been found, but most of them are known only from their radio emissions, and only a few have been identified with optical objects. Of these the most famous lies in the middle of the Crab Nebula, an expanding gas-patch in Taurus which was discovered in 1731 by the English astronomer John Bevis; it lies near the third-magnitude star Zeta Tauri, and good binoculars will

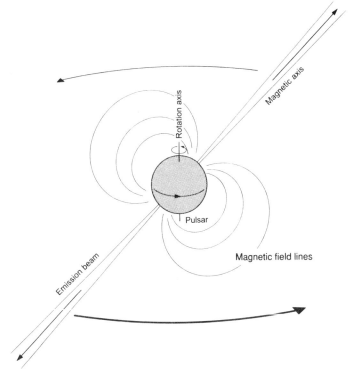

Pulsar diagram

show it, though a telescope is needed to bring out its form – the nickname was bestowed on it in 1845 by the Earl of Rosse, who looked at it through his great 72-inch reflector and thought that it gave a vague impression of a crustacean!

We know a great deal about the history of the Crab, because it is certainly the remnant of a supernova which blazed out in 1054, and was carefully followed by star-gazers in China and Korea. It became as bright as Venus, so that it could be seen in broad daylight, and it remained a naked-eye object for months before fading away. A pulsar was located in it during the 1960s, and was then tracked down to a very faint, flashing object which is visible only with very sensitive equipment. There is no doubt about the identification, because both the 'flasher' and the pulsar have the same period; one-thirtieth of a second.

As a pulsar ages it slows down, and loses energy. This slowing-down can be measured, gradual though it is, and there are also 'glitches' or irregularities, due possibly to tremendous disturbances in the crust of the neutron star. Eventually, no doubt, the rotation will stop and the pulsar will cease to pulse, but again we are by no means sure that there has been sufficient time for this to happen. No pulsar is known with a period or more than five seconds.

To digress briefly: we also find pulsars which spin much more quickly than the Crab, at rates of hundreds of times per second. Apparently these are not young, but are old neutron stars which have been 'spun up'. A millisecond pulsar is thought to be the neutron-star component of a binary system, of which the other member is a huge, distended red giant. The neutron star pulls material away from the giant, and when the material hits the surface of the neutron star it increases the speed of rotation; (you can demonstrate the effect by suspending a table-tennis ball on the end of a string and blowing on it through a straw). The giant suffers badly during this process, and in one case, a system in the constellation of Sagitta, we have a pulsar which is spinning 642 times per second and is actually evaporating its luckless companion, which will ultimately disappear completely. Not surprisingly, the attacking pulsar has been nicknamed the Black Widow!

Of course, not all neutron stars show up as pulsars, because we will not be able to detect the beams of radiation unless they sweep across us. Neither are we absolutely certain that all Type II supernovae produce pulsars, though all the evidence points that way.

Only four supernovae have been definitely recorded in our Galaxy during the past thousand years – those of 1006, 1054, 1572 (Tycho's Star) and 1604 (Kepler's Star), and of these only that of 1054 was a Type II. It is impossible to predict when we will see another; perhaps the best candidate is Eta Carinae, which is very massive and highly unstable and will definitely 'go supernova' eventually, though this may not happen for a great many centuries. At least a naked-eye supernova was seen in 1987, when it blazed out in the Large Cloud of Magellan and became very prominent even though it was 169,000 light-years away. We are still waiting for a pulsar to show itself, but so far nothing has happened.

In 1991 British radio astronomers reported that slight irregularities in the behaviour of one particular pulsar, PSR 1829-10, indicated that it was attended by a planet about ten times as massive as the Earth. This sounded wildly improbable, because the region of a pulsar is the very last place where one would expect to find a planet, and it did indeed turn out to be a mistake, but since then there have been claims from America of other 'pulsar planets'. I am highly sceptical, because if a pulsar is the result of a supernova outburst no planetary body could possibly survive. There have also been reports of planets round 'normal' stars, such as 51 Pegasi which is 42 light-years away and slightly less luminous than the Sun; another candidate is 47 Ursae Majoris, about the same distance from us but a little more luminous than the Sun. These claims are based on slight 'wobblings' of the visible stars, in which case the hypothetical planets must be more Jupiter-like than Earth-like in mass. Again I tend to be sceptical, but again we must wait and see. Probably the best 'bet' so far is Beta Pictoris, where the surrounding material has actually been seen, and may well be deformed in a way which indicates the presence of a large orbiting planet.

Let us now come back to stellar evolution, and consider the case of a star which is too massive even to explode as a Type II supernova. Here it seems that once the grand collapse starts, nothing can stop it; it is too cataclysmic. Gravitation takes over, and as the star becomes smaller and smaller, and denser and denser, the escape velocity rises, finally reaching the value of 186,000 miles per second. This is the speed of light. Not even light can now break free from the star, which has now surrounded itself with a 'forbidden zone' from which nothing – absolutely nothing – can escape. It has become a black hole.

The boundary of the black hole is termed the event horizon. If the Sun became a black hole, the diameter of the event horizon would be about four miles; for the Earth, less than an inch. Yet there is no chance the Sun or the Earth will create black holes; even the Sun is not nearly massive enough, and is fated to end its luminous career much more sedately as a white dwarf.

Obviously we cannot see a black hole, but we can locate it indirectly. The best candidate is a system known as Cygnus X-1, in the Swan, which is 6500 light-years away. It is made up of a very luminous B-type supergiant, with a diameter of at least 12,000,000 miles and a mass thirty times that of the Sun, together with a companion which is fourteen times as massive as the Sun; the companion has never been

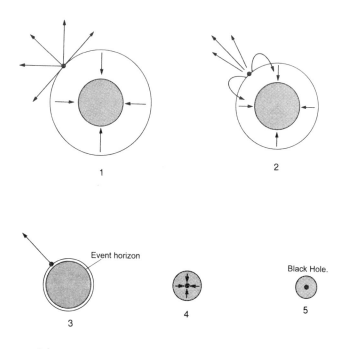

Formation of a black hole. 1. Light visible from surface as star begins to collapse. 2. As collapse accelerates some light rays are bent back. 3. As star approaches the Schwarzchild radius only vertical light rays escape. 4. When star collapses inside radius it vanishes from view. 5. Star falls into singularity.

seen, but betrays its presence by its gravitational pull on the super-giant. The elusive companion is too massive to be a neutron star, and is presumably a black hole. It is drawing material away from the luminous star, and before this material is sucked over the event horizon, to vanish forever, it is so strongly heated that it gives off X-rays which we can pick up – hence the name Cygnus X-1. We cannot be absolutely sure that this is the correct explanation, but it is over-whelmingly probable, and various other black hole candidates have been found. Confirmation has come, too, from the Hubble Space Telescope, which has been used to study the movement of material inside a galaxy known as M.87. The way in which this material is moving shows that it must be under the influence of an invisible body of immense mass, and this again seems to point to the existence of a black hole. Indeed, very recent research with the Hubble Space Telescope indicates that with any large galaxy, a central black hole may be the rule rather than the exception.

A black hole is the weirdest object that we can imagine. What happens inside the event horizon we do not know; does the collapsed star crush itself out of existence altogether? Exotic theories – such as the idea of entering a black hole and emerging in a different part of the universe, or in a different universe altogether – are entertaining, but so speculative that further discussion of them is really rather pointless.

We have learned a great deal during the past few decades, and we are finding out more all the time. There are still many aspects of stellar evolution which puzzle us, but one thing is definite: no star can shine for ever, and it has a limited life-span, even though it may take thousands of millions of years to evolve from a mass of cool gas into a white dwarf, a neutron star or a black hole.

# 16

# STAR-CLUSTERS AND NEBULAE

Look up into the evening sky at any time around Christmas, and you cannot fail to notice the 'haze' which makes up the star-cluster of the Pleiades, often known as the Seven Sisters. It has been known since prehistoric times, and almost every early civilisation has legends about it. Closer inspection shows that it is starry, and at least seven separate stars can be seen with the naked eye under normal conditions; keen-sighted people can distinguish more, and the record is said to be nineteen. Binoculars bring many more into view, and the total membership of the cluster amounts to several hundreds. There is no doubt that the clustering is genuine; the chances of the main stars being arranged in this way by sheer chance are many millions to one against, and in any case many other open or loose clusters are known. Other prominent examples are the Hyades, round Aldebaran; Praesepe in Cancer, the Crab; the Sword-Handle in Perseus (not to be be confused with the Sword of Orion); the lovely 'Wild Duck' cluster in Scutum, and the equally lovely 'Jewel Box' round Kappa Crucis in the far south.

Open clusters cannot maintain their identity permanently. They are not tightly bound systems, and so they are constantly perturbed by field stars in the Galaxy which are not members of the group and are travelling in different directions. Eventually the cluster will be dispersed, though of course the process is a very gradual one, and the rate depends upon the position in the Galaxy. Thus Messier 67, in Cancer, is well away from the main galactic plane, so that it is in a fairly sparsely populated region and there are fewer field stars to disrupt it, so that it is relatively old. Many of its stars are reddish, showing that they are well advanced in their life-stories and have left the Main Sequence; on the other hand the leaders of the Pleiades are hot, luminous and bluish-white, so that the age of the cluster cannot be more than a few millions of years.

Around a dozen clusters had been identified by the end of the seventeenth century, but the first really comprehensive catalogue was not drawn up before 1781. It was the work of a French astronomer, Charles Messier, who listed over a hundred objects and numbered them; thus the Pleiades cluster is Messier 45 (M.45), Praesepe is M.44, and so on. Ironically, Messier was not in the least interested in clusters or nebulae. He was a comet-hunter, and found that he was being constantly misled by dim objects which lay well beyond the Solar System. Finally he lost patience, and decided to compile a list of them as 'objects to avoid'. We still use Messier's catalogue, though none of the comets he discovered during his career proved to be of any particular interest! Much later, the Danish astronomer J. L. E. Dreyer drew up a much more elaborate catalogue, referred to as the NGC or New General Catalogue even though it is now over a century old. Both lists are in common use; thus Praesepe is known as NGC 2632 as well as M.44.

Both the Messier and NGC lists contain objects of various kinds, ranging from open clusters to globular clusters, nebulae, galaxies and even supernova remnants; the Crab Nebula is M.1 or NGC 1952. All the objects in Messier's catalogue are within the range of small telescopes, and identifying them is a pleasant pastime; though they are not easy to draw accurately, they are favourite targets for astronomical photographers. Of course they differ widely in size and prominence. Some of the clusters are rich, while others are poor and obscure; there are two Messier objects – numbers 40 and 91 – which are missing, and may be comets which were not identified at the time, while M.102 is generally thought to have been identical with M.101, a spiral galaxy in Ursa Major.

Large open clusters such as the Pleiades and the Hyades are probably best viewed with binoculars, because they are too spread out to be contained in the same telescopic field. The Pleiades cluster contains nebulosity, showing that there is still 'star-forming' material present; this nebulosity is not hard to photograph, but is very elusive visually. There is no nebulosity in the Hyades cluster, which was not listed by Messier – presumably because there was not the slightest chance of confusing it with a comet. Another absentee from Messier's catalogue is the Sword-Handle in Perseus, made up of two clusters in the same field. M.11, in Scutum, is fan-shaped, and has been nicknamed the 'Wild Duck', while Cancer contains two prominent clusters: M.44 (Praesepe), an easy naked-eye object, and M.67, which can be seen with binoculars. Praesepe, the 'Beehive', is bounded by two naked-eye stars, Delta and Gamma Cancri, which are known as the Aselli or Asses, since another nickname for Praesepe is the 'Manger' (it is not easy to see why the ancient Chinese referred to it as 'the exhalation of piled-up corpses'!). As we have noted, M.67 is exceptionally ancient by open cluster standards, because it lies well away from the plane of the Galaxy and has been left relatively undisturbed by passing non-cluster stars. In the Southern Cross we find the exquisite Jewel Box, with bluish-white stars and one prominent foreground red giant, while there are many other clusters within binocular range.

Open clusters have no particular shape, and seldom contain more than a few hundred stars. Globular clusters are quite different. They are huge, symmetrical systems, sometimes with more than a million members, lying round the edges of the main Galaxy. Only about a hundred are known in our own system, and only three are clearly visible with the naked eye: Omega Centauri and 47 Tucanae in the far south, and M.13 in Hercules. All globulars are very remote, which is why they look comparatively faint.

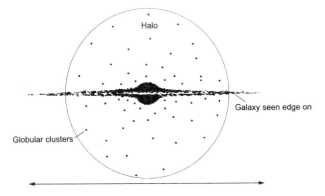

Distribution of globular clusters

Globular clusters are old, and have no nebulosity left. Their leading stars tend to be ancient red giants which have long since left the Main Sequence, but there are also Cepheid variables, and it was by studying these useful stars that Harlow Shapley, in 1917, was able to draw up the first good picture of the shape of the Galaxy. He could observe the periods of the Cepheids, and find out how far away they were; this meant that he also knew the distances of the globular clusters in which they lay. He also realised that the globulars are not distributed evenly around the sky, but are concentrated in the southern hemisphere, particularly in the region of Sagittarius. Shapley deduced – quite correctly – that this is because the Solar System lies not at the centre of the Galaxy, but well out toward one edge, so that we are having what amounts to a lop-sided view. We now know that the Sun is almost 30,000 light-years from the galactic centre, which lies beyond the Sagittarius star-clouds.

Telescopically, it is easy enough to resolve the edges of globular clusters into stars, but near the centre the stars are so closely packed that they seem to merge into a general mass; the average distance between stars in the heart of a globular is only a few light-days instead of several light-years. The sky as seen from a planet moving round a star in such a region would be ablaze, with many stars brilliant enough to cast shadows; there would be no proper darkness at all, and of course many of the brightest stars would be red. Yet an astronomer living near the centre of a globular cluster would be able to find out very little about the outer universe!

Much the brightest of the globulars is Omega Centauri, which shows up to the naked eye as a hazy object of about the fourth magnitude; it lies in the northern part of the Centaur (declination –47½ degrees) and Bayer gave it a Greek letter. It is one of the closer members of the class, but even so it is still 17,000 light-years away; the real diameter cannot be less than 150 light-years. Unfortunately it is too far south to be seen from Britain, and this is also true of its only rival, 47 Tucanae, which is almost silhouetted against the Small Cloud of Magellan. The best northern globular is M.13, between Eta and Zeta Herculis, which is a difficult naked-eye object but is very easy with binoculars, and was discovered in 1714 by no less a person than Edmond Halley. Its outer parts are easy to resolve, but oddly enough it is relatively poor in variable stars.

The most detailed views of the central regions of globular clusters have been obtained with the Hubble Space Telescope. In particular, it has been possible to identify what are termed 'blue stragglers', hot blue stars which logically ought not to be there; globular clusters are so ancient that all their leading stars should have left the Main Sequence by now. Apparently a blue straggler is formed when two stars approach each other closely enough to form a binary system, after which the more massive member draws material away from its more evolved, less dense companion – with the result that the main star heats up, becoming a blue giant again. Over twenty blue stragglers are known inside 47 Tucanae, of which eleven were found with the Hubble telescope in 1991. However, the results did not confirm a popular suggestion that lurking in the centre of a globular cluster there is likely to be a super-massive black hole.

Messier's catalogue includes several of the objects always known as planetary nebulae, though – as we have noted – the name is a bad one inasmuch as the objects concerned are not true nebulae and have absolutely nothing to do with planets. A planetary nebula is a very old star which has blown away its outer layers, so that it is surrounded by an extensive, very tenuous shell. When we look at this shell we see it at its brightest near the edges, giving the aspect of a ring round a small, very hot central star. The best-known planetary is the Ring Nebula, M.57, between Beta and Gamma Lyrae, near Vega. It is very hard to see with binoculars, but a small telescope shows it, and a larger instrument will reveal the central star; the overall appearance has been likened to a tiny, luminous cycle-tyre. Not all planetaries are as symmetrical as this; M.27, in Vulpecula (the Fox) earns its nickname of the Dumbbell, while two stars in the much fainter M.97, in Ursa Major, have led to its being generally known as the Owl.

One planetary nebula, Hen 1357, has actually been observed in the process of formation. (It is so called because it was the 1357th object in a list of unusual stars compiled by Karl Henize.) It is about 18,000 light-years away, and lies in the southern constellation of Ara, the Altar. When first noted by Henize it looked like an ordinary hot star, but in 1993 a picture taken by the Hubble Space Telescope revealed that it had blown away its outer shell and had taken on the aspect of a planetary nebula. In fact, the process may have started several thousands of years ago, but only recently has there been enough radiation from the star to make the ejected gas glow.

The Crab Nebula is the only supernova remnant in Messier's list (appropriately, it is lettered No.1), but there are a number of gaseous or galactic nebulae. The best-known is M.42, the Sword of Orion, which is 1500 light-years away and about 30 light-years in diameter.

It is a stellar nursery, and contains many very young stars which are still contracting toward the Main Sequence, so that they are flickering irregularly. We cannot see through to the heart of M.42, but infra-red radiation is not blocked by the nebular material, and we know that deep inside the 'Sword' there are some very massive young stars which we will never be able to observe directly; they will not live for long enough to 'burn a hole' and show themselves.

Nebulae shine because they are being lit up by hot stars in or very near them. Some nebulae shine purely by reflection, but in other cases the very hot stars ionise the hydrogen and make it emit light on its own account, which is why these emission nebulae are also termed H.II regions. M.42 is only the brightest part of a vast molecular cloud covering most of Orion. The four stars of the Trapezium, Theta Orionis, lie near the edge of the Earth-turned side of the nebula, and it is these stars which make the 'Sword' shine. Among other conspicuous nebulae are the Lagoon (M.8) and the Trifid (M.20) in Sagittarius, and the nebulosity surrounding the erratic southern variable Eta Carinae.

But suppose that there are no convenient stars to make the material shine – what then? The answer is that the nebulosity will remain dark, and will be detectable only because it blots out the light of stars beyond. The most famous of all dark nebulae is the Coal Sack, in the Southern Cross, which covers almost thirty square degrees and looks like a starless area (or nearly so; there are a few faint foreground stars showing up against the blackness). Another dark nebula, near Alnitak in Orion's Belt, is known as the Horse's Head because its shape recalls that of a knight in chess; it is very hard to see visually; even with a large telescope, but it is not difficult to photograph, and it stands out clearly against the bright nebulosity surrounding it. In Cygnus we can locate dark rifts in the Milky Way, and these too are due to obscuring material.

There is no difference between a bright nebula and a dark one – except for the presence or absence of illuminating stars. For all we know, there may be a 'Trapezium' on the far side of the Coal Sack which will light up the regions turned away from us; if we were observing from another point in the Galaxy, it might be the Coal Sack which would look bright and Orion's Sword which would remain dark. At least there is plenty of variety in the Galaxy!

# 17

# THE DEPTHS — OF THE UNIVERSE —

In this light-polluted era there must be many people who have never seen the Milky Way, but against a clear, dark sky it is magnificent, and it must have been known ever since the dawn of human history; every country has a store of legends about it. It was Sir William Herschel who first set out to determine the shape of the Galaxy, and he who realised that the Milky Way is nothing more than a line of sight effect. He came to the conclusion that the Galaxy must be shaped like 'a cloven grindstone', which is not so very far from the truth, but its size was not measured until Harlow Shapley's work carried out from Mount Wilson in 1917.

As we have noted, the Sun lies almost 30,000 light-years from the galactic centre, and we also know that the Galaxy is rotating; the Sun takes 225,000,000 years to complete one circuit – a period often called the 'cosmic year'. One cosmic year ago, the most advanced life-forms on Earth were amphibians; even the dinosaurs lay in the future. It is interesting to speculate as to what conditions here may be like one cosmic year hence!

What we cannot do is to see right through to the centre of the Galaxy. We know where it is; it lies beyond the lovely star-clouds in Sagittarius, but it is hidden by the 'dust' which lies in the way. Fortunately, there are other methods of investigation. Infra-red radiation is not blocked by the dust, and neither are radio waves, so that we can learn at least something about conditions in the heart of the Galaxy. There is a strong radio source, known as Sagittarius A-* (pronounced Sagittarius A-star) which may indicate a massive black hole, though its exact nature is still in doubt; at any rate, it is very near the central point.

We also know that the Galaxy is spiral in form. The first evidence here came from radio astronomy, not long after the end of the Second World War. There are clouds of cold hydrogen spread through the Galaxy, and these give off radio emissions at a wavelength of 21.1 cm. Plotting the distribution of these clouds confirmed that there are spiral arms, and that the Sun lies near the edge of one of them. There is nothing at all surprising in this, and neither is there anything exceptional about our own Galaxy.

How far can you see with the naked eye? Asked this question, most people will reply 'Oh! – a few miles.' In fact the answer is 'around 12 million million million miles', because this is the distance of M.31, the Andromeda Spiral, which is about 2.2 million light-years away and is the most remote object which can be clearly seen without optical aid. But for a long time its nature was not realised.

The nebulae in Messier's catalogue were of two distinct types. Some, such as M.42 in Orion's Sword, looked like masses of gas; others, such as M.31, gave every impression of being 'starry'. Nobody could be sure whether the starry nebulae were members of the Milky Way, or whether they were independent systems – 'island universes' – at much greater distances. In 1845 the third Earl of Rosse, using his home-made 72-inch reflecting telescope at Birr Castle in Ireland, saw that many of the starry nebulae were spiral in form, like Catherine-wheels, though others were circular, elliptical or even irregular in shape. Certainly they were quite different from the gas-patches, but everything depended upon how far away they were.

The problem was solved in 1923 by Edwin Hubble, again using the Mount Wilson 100-inch telescope. He knew about the Cepheid period-luminosity law established years earlier by Miss Leavitt, and he set out to locate Cepheids in some of the spirals, including M.31. He found them, and measured their periods; this gave him their distances, and it was at once clear that they could not possibly be contained in our Galaxy. Hubble gave the distance of M.31 as 900,000 light-years, subsequently reduced to 750,000 light-years. This was one of the greatest discoveries in the history of astronomy, and it altered all our ideas about the universe. Just as the Earth had been found to be an unimportant planet and the Sun an unimportant star, so it now emerged that the Milky Way itself is an unimportant galaxy.

More was to follow. In 1952 Walter Baade used the then-new Palomar 200-inch reflector to show that there had been an error in the Cepheid scale. There are two kinds of short-period variables, one much more luminous than the other, and Hubble, through no fault of his own, had picked wrong. The variables which he had studied were of the more powerful type, and so the distance which he had given for M.31 was an underestimate; it had to be increased by a factor of more than two, and there were similar errors in the distance of the other

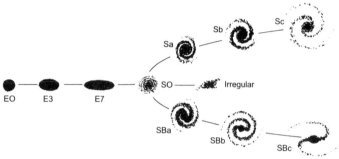

Hubble's tuning fork diagram

galaxies. In one short paper, delivered at a meeting of the Royal Astronomical Society in London, Baade calmly doubled the size of the universe.

But nothing could detract from the value of Edwin Hubble's work; it was he who made the great breakthrough. Together with his colleague Milton Humason (who began his Mount Wilson career as a mule driver, graduating to the rank of janitor and then to the status of one of the world's greatest astronomers!) Hubble drew up a classification of the external systems, based on their forms. The old term of 'spiral nebulae' was dropped, to be replaced by 'galaxies', while 'nebula' was taken to indicate a gas-and-dust cloud.

Hubble divided the galaxies into five main classes. First there were the spirals, some of which are truly beautiful; it is easy to see why M.51, in the little constellation of Canes Venatici (the Hunting Dogs) has been nicknamed the Whirlpool. M.31 is also spiral, but it lies at a narrow angle to us, so that the full effect is lost. There are various subdivisions, lettered a, b and c. Sa spirals have conspicuous, often tightly wound arms issuing from a well-defined nucleus; Sb systems have looser arms and less condensed nuclei, while in the Sc spirals the nucleus is inconspicuous and the arms are very loose indeed. Our Galaxy is of type Sb.

With barred spirals, the arms issue from the ends of a kind of 'bar' through the nucleus; they are subdivided into types SBa, SBb and SBc. Elliptical galaxies show no signs of spirality; they range from E7 (highly flattened) through to E0 (virtually spherical, and looking superficially very like globular clusters even though they are far more populous and massive). Finally there are the irregular galaxies, with no definite form. It is now thought that about 30 per cent of galaxies are spiral, 60 per cent elliptical and 10 per cent irregular, though these figures are very approximate.

It was natural to think that spirals should evolve into ellipticals, or vice versa, but this does not seem to be true. More probably the final form depends upon the initial mass of the galaxy concerned. Neither does it seem that spiral arms are permanent. 'Pressure waves' sweep round the system and compress the material, triggering off star formation; this means that in a spiral galaxy the arms will always exist – but they will not always be the same arms, or in the same positions.

It cannot honestly be said that galaxies are spectacular objects when observed visually, even in large telescopes; the best results are obtained photographically, or today with electronic equipment. However, we can at least see that the galaxies contain all the various types of objects with which we are familiar in the Milky Way. There are open and globular clusters, planetaries, gaseous nebulae, variable stars and novae; supernovae flare up from time to time, and their immense power means that they can be seen across great distances. In recent years some amateur astronomers have concentrated upon hunting for supernovae in outer galaxies, and have a fine record of success.

Our Galaxy is a member of what is termed the Local Group, which includes a few large systems and more than two dozen of smaller size. The closest of the important systems are the two Clouds of Magellan, which are less than 200,000 light-years away, and so can be studied in great detail. At a greater distance come M.31, the Andromeda

Spiral, and the smaller spiral M.33 in Triangulum. There may be another major member of the group: Maffei 1, but we know little about it, because it lies near the main plane of the Milky Way and is heavily obscured. A spiral galaxy, also heavily obscured, was discovered in 1994 from Holland, but may be just beyond the Local Group.

The junior members of the Local Group are real dwarfs, some of which are hardly more populous than globular clusters and have no definite shape. The closest of them – and, indeed, the closest of all the external systems – is a dwarf in Sagittarius, discovered in 1994 by Rodriga Ibata and his colleagues working at Cambridge. It is about 80,000 light-years away from us, but lies on the far side of the Galaxy, and is no more than 50,000 light-years from the galactic centre. It – like the Clouds of Magellan – is a satellite of our Galaxy, but unlike the Clouds it is being gravitationally disrupted, and over the next few hundred million years it will be absorbed into our Galaxy and will lose its separate identity.

The Local Group is stable, and indeed M.31 is actually approaching us at the present time, though this will not continue indefinitely. Collisions can, and do, occur, and the Hubble Space Telescope has found indications of a double nucleus in M.31 which may indicate the remnant of a smaller system which was absorbed long ago – though this is only one interpretation, and we cannot be sure.

Beyond the Local Group we come to other groups or clusters of galaxies, many of them far larger than ours; the Virgo cluster, at around 50,000,000 light-years, contains many hundreds of members, notably the giant elliptical M.87, which is also a strong source of radio waves (radio astronomers call it Virgo A). The Virgo cluster is probably the hub of a vast collection of systems known as the Local Supercluster. But all the groups are racing away from us, and from each other. This means that the entire universe is expanding.

Well before Hubble began his work, Vesto Slipher at the Lowell Observatory had made an important discovery. He found that apart from the systems contained in what we now know to be the Local Group, all the galaxies showed red shifts in their spectra – and assuming that these were Doppler effects, it followed that all the galaxies were receding. When Hubble measured their distances, it became clear that we are in no privileged position, and the expansion really is universal.

Cepheids are invaluable in measuring the distances of the closer galaxies, but with more remote systems the individual variables fade into the general background, and we must think again. We can use supergiant stars, assuming that the most luminous stars in other galaxies are of around the same power as the most luminous stars in the Milky Way; we can also use supernovae. But eventually even the supernovae are lost, and we come back to the spectral red shift. Find the speed of recession, and from this make an estimate of the distance. Though uncertainties are bound to creep in, it seems that the most remote systems known are at least 13,000 million light-years away, and are receding at well over 90 per cent of the velocity of light.

But, a note of caution here! Some astronomers, notably Halton Arp and Sir Fred Hoyle, believe that the red shifts are not pure Doppler shifts, and that there is a major non-velocity component. This is based on the undeniable fact that some systems, joined by luminous 'bridges' of material, seem to be associated with each other, and yet have completely different red shifts. If this interpretation is valid, then all our distance-measurements beyond our own immediate region of the Galaxy are unreliable, and many of our cherished theories will have to be either modified or else abandoned. Perhaps naturally, this is a distinctly unpopular view among astronomers as a whole, but the observational data have to be explained somehow or other. For the moment, however, let us be conventional – even though I have the feeling that in the long run Arp will prove to be right!

By 1963 radio astronomy had come very much to the fore, and catalogues of radio sources had been drawn up, notably by the Cambridge astronomers. The main problem was in identifying the sources with optical objects; in those days, radio telescopes were not nearly so accurate as they are now. For once Nature was helpful. A strong source, 3C-273 (the 273rd object in the third Cambridge catalogue) was occulted by the Moon, and this gave its position very precisely, so that it could be tracked down to what looked like a faint blue star. When the optical spectrum was examined, initially by Maarten Schmidt at Palomar, astronomers received a rude shock. 3C-273 was not a star at all, but something much more dramatic. The spectrum was totally unstellar, and showed hydrogen lines with a tremendous red shift. This meant that the object was very remote and immensely powerful; yet it looked small. How could so much energy come from so limited an area? If the red shift gave a real key to the distance, this first 'quasar', or quasi-stellar object, was much more powerful than any normal galaxy.

Other quasars were soon found, and by now hundreds are known, though by no means all of them are radio emitters. There seems little doubt that they are the nuclei of very active galaxies, probably powered by super-massive central black holes, and it may be that many galaxies go through a temporary quasar stage during their evolution; there is almost certainly a gradation between quasars, the so-called BL Lacertae objects (which are rather less luminous) and other galaxies which are quite different in appearance from quasars, but are very powerful at radio wavelengths. It has even been suggested that the three classes of objects may be of the same type, seen from different angles.

Quasars are so luminous that they can be seen out to distances at which normal galaxies have faded into invisibility. In some cases they show multiple images – not because they are really made up of separate components, but because their light passes close by a foreground galaxy which acts as a lens, and produces several images of the same quasar. Such is the so-called 'clover-leaf', where there are four images of the background quasar surrounding the intervening galaxy which is responsible for the lens effect.

All this means that we can now study the distribution of the galaxies in space, and initial results have been decidedly unexpected. There is a definite large-scale structure, with 'walls', super-clusters, and also vast voids which are only sparsely populated. But there is also a tremendous amount of material which we cannot see, and this brings us on to one of the most pressing problems of modern cosmology: that of the so-called missing mass.

A galaxy such as our own is rotating, with the individual stars moving round the centre of the system. According to Kepler's Laws, the closer-in stars should move the fastest, as with the planets in the Solar System; but this does not happen, and the orbital speeds do not fall away in Keplerian fashion. The only conclusion must be that the mass of the galaxy is not concentrated in the centre of the system, and that there is a great deal of invisible material. This also explains why the clusters of galaxies retain their separate identities; there is insufficient visible matter to make them stable, and so 'dark matter' must be involved.

It has even been calculated that the visible material in the universe – planets, stars, galaxies, everything – accounts for no more than 10 per cent of the total mass. All the rest is undetectable.

What can it be? Is it locked up in innumerable black holes? Are there swarms of stars so feeble that they do not show themselves? Or is the dark matter of a nature completely alien to us, so that our present-day equipment has no hope of detecting it? As yet we do not know, but the problem is of fundamental importance when we come to consider the past and future of the universe. In particular, we want to decide whether the present expansion will continue indefinitely, or whether there is sufficient mass to bring the expansion to a halt; and this leads on to the question of how the universe was created in the first place.

There are two alternatives. Either the universe was born at a definite moment in time, or else it has always existed, so that it has an infinite past. Neither concept is at all easy to grasp. We cannot visualise a period of time which had no beginning, and in any case this is no help in trying to understand how the material came into being; the one inescapable fact is that we exist, so that the atoms and molecules making up everything in the universe must have come from somewhere or other. If we adopt the other alternative, and assume that the universe began with a 'Big Bang' around 15,000 million years ago, we have to ask ourselves what happened at a still earlier period. All we can really say is that if space, time and matter all began at the same instant, there was no 'before'.

Observational evidence is against the 'steady-state' picture, and at least if we begin with a Big Bang we can work through a complete sequence of events, ending up with you and me. The universe was born; it was very small and incredibly hot, but we cannot say 'where' the Big Bang happened, because if space were created at the same moment then the Big Bang happened 'everywhere'. Expansion began – very rapidly at first, in what is termed the inflationary period – and then more slowly. The temperature fell; complex atoms formed from the original hydrogen, and in time galaxies were produced, followed by stars, planets, and – in the case of the Earth – life.

From the present rate of expansion, we can calculate that the Big Bang occurred between 15,000 million and 20,000 million years ago, with a marked preference for the lower value. Evidence also comes from weak radio emissions reaching us from all directions all the time, indicating an overall temperature for the universe of about three degrees above zero (absolute zero being the coldest temperature there can possibly be: −273°C). Presumably this is the last detectable manifestation of the Big Bang. If the original universe had begun to expand smoothly, it is not easy to see how galaxies could have been formed, but in 1993 a specially designed satellite, COBE (the Cosmic Background Explorer) was able to detect slight irregularities in the weak radiation, so that another major objection to the Big Bang theory was removed.

When we ask just how the Big Bang was caused, we are forced to admit our total ignorance, because all the ordinary laws of science break down. I have compared this with the plight of an intelligent being from Outer Space who arrives on Earth for a brief visit and spends half and hour in a busy street. He will see babies, boys, men and old men. If he is clever enough, he will realise that a baby turns into a boy and a boy into a man, so that he will be able to work out the evolutionary cycle of a human being − but unless someone has told him about the facts of life, he will not know how the baby appeared. In cosmology, our 'baby' is the Big Bang.

Whether the overall expansion will continue indefinitely is something else which we do not know, and again we come back to the question of the average density of matter in the universe. If the mass exceeds a certain critical value, the expansion will stop; the galaxies will start to rush together again, and in perhaps 80,000 million years there will be another Big Bang, so that the cycle can be repeated. If the total mass is too low, then there will be no return, and the expansion will go on until all the groups of galaxies have lost contact with each other. In the first scenario, the universe resembles a clock which is being regularly re-wound; in the second, it is like a clock which has been wound once and is now running down, so that eventually it will stop.

We are equally insecure when we consider the full size of the universe. Is it 'finite but unbounded'? However, we do have one clue. If the rule of 'the further, the faster' holds good, we will come to a distance at which a system will be receding at the full velocity of light; we will then be unable to see it, and we will have come to the boundary of the observable universe, though not necessarily of the universe itself. It seems that the limiting distance is around 15,000 million light-years.

There are hopes that the rejuvenated Hubble Space Telescope may take us to the 'outer limit', but for the moment we can do no more than wait and see.

In fact, in 1994 the Hubble Telescope did provide some new data which were rather surprising. A very accurate measurement of the distance of the galaxy M.100, in the Virgo Cluster, together with its rate of recession, indicated that the Big Bang must have happened more recently than has been believed. If so, then the age of the universe must be less than 12,000 million years. In this case, the oldest stars must be younger than this – one can hardly have stars which are older than the universe! As yet we cannot claim to have anything like a complete knowledge of the evolution of the universe.

We have come a long way since the time, not so very long ago, when the Earth was regarded as the centre of the entire universe, with everything in the sky produced for our sole benefit. Yet we are still woefully weak on fundamentals, and we cannot pretend that we have made much progress in understanding the most important problem of all – that of the Creation. One day, perhaps, we may find out.

# 18
## INTO THE
## FUTURE

In 1991 a General Assembly of the International Astronomical Union, the controlling body of world astronomy, was held at Buenos Aires, in Argentina. One meeting was of unusual interest. It dealt with the possibility of ETI, or Extra-Terrestrial Intelligence. Does it exist, and what action should we take if we found any evidence of it? After all, the Sun is a very normal star, one of 100,000 million in our Galaxy alone, and it does not seem logical to believe that it is unique in being attended by a peopled planet. But we must beware of jumping to conclusions, and we first have to decide what form any ETI is likely to take.

We may not know a great deal about 'life', but we do know a great deal about the properties of living matter, and it seems that the essential ingredient is carbon, because only the carbon atom has the ability to link up with other atoms to form the large, complicated molecules necessary for life. (Silicon is the only possible competitor, but it is not very efficient, and the chances of silicon-based life anywhere seem to be low.) We are therefore entitled to assume that life, wherever it may be found, will be carbon-based. If this is wrong, then almost all of our modern science is wrong too, and few people will be prepared to accept this.

If there is a planet like the Earth, orbiting a star like the Sun, there might well be Earth-type life; and if it has developed in the same way as our own, there could be a distinct chance of contacting it. Interstellar travel is out of the question in our present state of technology, if only because it would take far too long, and when we consider devices such as interstellar arks, space-warps, time-warps, teleportation and thought-travel we enter the realm of science fiction. So if we are to establish contact with other civilisations, the only feasible way seems to be by radio, since radio waves are electromagnetic vibrations and travel at the same speed as light.

The first serious attempt was made in 1960 by astronomers at Green Bank, in West Virginia. Using the powerful radio telescope there, they 'listened out' at a selected wavelength, 21.1 cm, hoping to pick up signals rhythmical enough to be interpreted as artificial. This wavelength was chosen because it is the frequency sent out by clouds of cold hydrogen in the Galaxy, and radio astronomers anywhere would be expected to pay particular attention to it. Not surprisingly, the results were negative, and the experiment was discontinued; later attempts were no more successful. Yet although the chances of picking up artificial transmissions are slight, they are not nil.

The first thing to do is to decide where to search. We know that there are stars associated with clouds of cool material which may be planet-forming; Vega is one, Fomalhaut another – but most of these stars are hot and white. So too is the most promising candidate of all, Beta Pictoris, where the cool material has actually been photographed. But Beta Pictoris is 78 light-years away, and we really need a star which is much more like our Sun. The two nearest candidates, Tau Ceti and Epsilon Eridani, are each about 11 light-years away. Admittedly both are rather smaller and cooler than the Sun, but they were logical targets for the first serious research programme.

We have no proof that planets exist there, but – why not? What can happen to the Sun can happen to other stars also. When we believed that the planets of our Solar System were pulled off the Sun by the action of a passing star, it was thought that planetary systems must be uncommon, because close encounters between stars are so rare, at least in our part of the Galaxy; but now that we have come round to the solar nebula picture, there is every reason to think that planetary families may abound. This view was strengthened in 1983 by the career of IRAS, the Infra-Red Astronomical Satellite, which detected a large number of stars with cool surrounds.

When it comes to sending or receiving messages, the only possible procedure is to use the language of mathematics. We did not invent mathematics; we merely discovered it, and it is universal. If we could receive a signal rhythmical enough to be classed as non-natural, we would have proved our point.

The time-delay is always going to be a problem. If, say, we send a message to Tau Ceti in 1995, it will arrive in 2006. Assuming that an obliging radio astronomer there hears it and sends a prompt reply, we will receive our answer in 2017 – a total delay of 22 years. Unfortunately, there seems to be nothing we can do about this.

There is always the chance that some other civilisation has mastered the art of interstellar travel, and will pay us a visit. There is not the slightest evidence that this has happened yet, and we can totally discount the flying saucer craze which has been rampant ever since the late 1940s, but it is quite true that contact of this kind is not absolutely out of the question. If it ever happens, there will be no cause for alarm, because any civilisation advanced enough to travel between the stars will long since have abandoned childish pursuits such as warfare. Frankly, I would welcome such a visit. I am quite sure that such a civilisation could teach us a great deal!

There may be races of all kinds in the Galaxy, from Stone Age cultures through to brilliant civilisations far ahead of ours both morally and technologically. There may also be ruined, radioactive planets whose inhabitants have wiped each other out – and we can only hope that this is a fate which we on Earth will be sensible enough to avoid.

Finally, what are the possibilities of an exotic form of space-travel to which the speed of light is no barrier? At the moment we have no idea of how this might be achieved. It would require some fundamental breakthrough which may come either in the foreseeable future, the far future, or never. Science fiction does have a habit of turning into science fact, and it is worth commenting that television or even radio would have seemed hopelessly fantastic at the time of the Armada; but at the moment, speculation about this sort of travel is not only endless but also rather pointless.

There are still a few astronomers who maintain that we really are unique, and that there is no other life anywhere in the cosmos. They may be right, but I doubt it – and in my personal view there is a strong chance that at this very moment, somewhere in the Galaxy, there is an author who is considering the same problem, and wondering whether there can be any intelligent life on a planet moving round the yellow dwarf star which we call the Sun.

# GLOSSARY

**Absolute magnitude** The apparent magnitude which a star would have if it could be viewed from a standard distance of 10 parsecs, or 32.6 light-years.

**Albedo** The reflecting power of a planet or other body. For example, the average albedo of the Moon is 7 per cent, so that it reflects 7 per cent of the sunlight falling upon it.

**Aphelion** The furthest distance of a planet or other body from the Sun in its orbit.

**Apogee** The furthest point of the Moon from the Earth in its orbit. The term also applies to any other body orbiting the Earth, such as an artificial satellite.

**Apparent magnitude** The apparent brightness of a celestial body. The lower the magnitude, the brighter the object.

**Astronomical unit** The mean distance of the Earth from the Sun. It is equal to 92,976,000 miles or 149,598,500 kilometres.

**Aurora** Aurorae are polar lights; aurora borealis in the northern hemisphere, aurora australis in the southern. They are due to charged particles from the Sun which enter the upper air.

**Azimuth** The bearing of an object in the sky, from north (0 degrees) through east, south and west.

**Barycentre** The centre of gravity of the Earth–Moon system. Since the Earth is 81 times as massive as the Moon, the barycentre lies well inside the Earth's globe.

**Binary star** A stellar system made up of two (or more) components which are physically associated.

**Black hole** A region round a very small, super-massive collapsed star from which not even light can escape.

**Caldera** A very large volcanic crater.

**Cassegrain reflector** A reflecting telescope in which the secondary mirror is convex, and the light is passed to the eyepiece via a hole in the centre of the main mirror.

**Celestial sphere** An imaginary sphere surrounding the Earth, whose centre is coincident with that of the Earth's globe.

**Cepheid** A short-period, very regular variable star.

**Chromosphere** That part of the Sun's atmosphere which lies above the bright surface or photosphere. The dark Fraunhofer lines of the solar spectrum are produced in the chromosphere.

**Circumpolar star** A star which never sets from the latitude of the observer.

**Coelostat** A clock-driven mirror on an axis parallel to the Earth's, so as to reflect the same region of the sky continuously.

**Colures** Great circles on the celestial sphere.

**Coma** The nebulous envelope of the head of a comet.

**Conjunction** 1. The close approach in the sky of two celestial bodies. 2. For the inferior planets, inferior conjunction occurs when the planet passes approximately between the Earth and the Sun, and superior conjunction when it is directly on the far side of the Sun. Planets beyond the Earth's orbit can reach superior conjunction only.

**Corona** The outermost part of the Sun's atmosphere.

**Cosmic rays** High-speed atomic particles reaching the Earth from outer space.

**Culmination** The maximum altitude of a celestial body above the horizon.

**Day, Sidereal** The interval between successive culminations of the same star: 23h 56m 4.091s.

**Day, Solar** The mean interval between successive culminations of the Sun; it is longer than the sidereal day because of the Sun's eastward motion. Its mean length is 24h 3m 56.555s.

**Declination** The angular distance of a celestial body north or south of the celestial equator.

**Dichotomy** The exact half-phase of the Moon or an inferior planet.

**Doppler effect** The apparent change in wavelength of a light-source according to its motion relative to the observer.

**Earthshine** The faint luminosity of the non-sunlit part of the Moon, due to light reflected on to the Moon from the Earth.

**Eclipse, Lunar** The passage of the full moon through the shadow cast by the Earth. Lunar eclipses may be total, partial or penumbral.

**Eclipse, Solar** The occultation of the Sun by the Moon. Solar eclipses may be total, partial or annular (an annular eclipse occurs with the Moon in the far part of its orbit, so that its disk then appears smaller than that of the Sun).

**Ecliptic** The apparent yearly path of the Sun among the stars, i.e. the projection of the Earth's orbit on to the celestial sphere.

**Equator, Celestial** The projection of the Earth's equator on to the celestial sphere: declination 0 degrees.

**Equatorial mounting for a telescope** A mounting in which the telescope is set up on a polar axis which is parallel to the axis of rotation of the Earth.

**Equinox** The points where the ecliptic cuts the celestial equator. The vernal equinox (First Point of Aries) is now in Pisces, and the autumnal equinox (First Point of Libra) in Virgo. The Sun crosses the vernal equinox in later March and the autumnal equinox in late September.

**Escape velocity** The minimum velocity needed for a body to escape from the surface of a planet (or other body) without extra impetus; in the case of the Earth, 7 miles per second.

**Extinction** The apparent reduction in light of a celestial body depending upon its altitude above the horizon.

**Eyepiece (or Ocular)** The lens, or combination of lenses, at the eye-end of a telescope, responsible for all the actual magnification of the image.

**Faculae** Bright patches on the surface of the Sun.

**Flare, Solar** A brilliant, energetic outbreak above the Sun's surface.

**Galaxies** Systems of stars.

**Gamma-rays** Ultra-short-wave radiations.

**Gegenschein (English, Counterglow)** A faint glow in the sky exactly opposite to the Sun. It is due to the illumination of interplanetary material in the main plane of the Solar System.

**Gibbous phase** The phase of the Moon or a planet between half and full.

**Great circle** A circle on the surface of a sphere whose plane passes through the centre of that sphere.

**Gregorian reflector** An obsolete form of reflecting telescope which has a concave secondary mirror, the light being passed to the eyepiece through a hole in the centre of the main mirror.

**Hertzsprung–Russell Diagram** A diagram in which stars are plotted according to their spectral types and their luminosities.

**Hour angle** The time which has elapsed since the culmination of a celestial object.

**Hour circle** A great circle on the celestial sphere which passes through both the celestial poles.

**Inferior planets** Mercury and Venus, which are closer to the Sun than we are.

**Infra-red radiation** Light of wavelength longer than that of visible light, but shorter than that of radio waves.

**Julian day** A count of the days, reckoned from 1 January 4713 BC.

**Kiloparsec** One thousand parsecs (3260 light-years).

**Libration** The apparent 'tilting' of the Moon as seen from the Earth.

**Light-year** The distance travelled by light in one year: 5.880 million million miles or 9.4607 million million kilometres.

**Local group** The group of galaxies of which our Galaxy is a member.

**Lunation** The interval between successive new moons: 29d 12h 44m.

**Magnetosphere** The region of the magnetic field round a celestial body.

**Main sequence** A band across the Hertzsprung–Russell Diagram running from top left to lower right. It includes the vast majority of stars.

**Maksutov telescope** A telescope involving both mirrors and lenses.

**Megaparsec** One million parsecs.

**Meridian, Celestial** The great circle on the celestial sphere which passes through the zenith and both celestial poles.

**Meteor** A piece of cometary debris; a small particle which burns away in the Earth's upper air, producing the effect known as a shooting-star.

**Meteorite** A solid body which lands on Earth. Meteorites come from the asteroid belt, and are not associated with comets or meteors.

**Micron (μ)** One-thousandth of a millimetre.

**Minor planet (or Asteroid)** A small planetary body; most asteroids move in the region of the Solar System between the orbits of Mars and Jupiter.

**Nebula** A cloud of dust and gas in space.

**Neutron** A fundamental particle with no electrical charge, but a mass equal to that of a proton.

**Neutrino** A particle with no electrical charge and no mass (or at least very little).

**Neutron star** The remnant of a supernova outburst; the core of a disrupted star, now made up of neutrons.

**Newtonian reflector** A reflecting telescope in which the light is collected by a curved mirror, and directed to the eyepiece via a secondary flat mirror inclined at an angle of 45 degrees.

**Nodes** The points at which the orbit of the Moon, a planet or a comet cuts the plane of the ecliptic.

**Nova** The sudden, temporary outburst of a formerly faint star. All novae are binary systems.

**Obliquity of the ecliptic** The angle between the ecliptic and the celestial equator: 23°26′45″.

**Occultation** The covering-up of one celestial body by another.

**Opposition** The position of a planet when exactly opposite to the Sun in the sky.

**Orbit** The path of a celestial body.

**Parallax, Trigonometrical** The apparent shift of an object against its background when viewed from different directions.

**Parsec** The distance at which a star would have a parallax of one second of arc: 3.26 light-years. (No star apart from the Sun is as close as this.)

**Penumbra** 1. The area of partial shadow to either side of the main cone of shadow cast by the Earth. 2. The lighter part of a sunspot.

**Perigee** The position of the Moon when closest to the Earth in its orbit. The term also applies to any other body in Earth orbit, such as an artificial satellite.

**Perihelion** The position of a planet or other body when closest to the Sun in its orbit.

**Photon** The smallest 'unit' of light.

**Photosphere** The bright surface of the Sun.

**Planetary nebula** A small, dense, hot star surrounded by a shell of gas. It is neither a planet nor a true nebula!

**Poles, Celestial** The north and south points of the celestial sphere.

**Position angle** The apparent direction of one object with reference to another, measured from the north point of the main object through east, south and west.

**Precession** The apparent slow movement of the celestial poles, due to the changing direction of the Earth's axis of rotation.

**Prime meridian** The meridian on the Earth's surface which passes through Greenwich Observatory. It marks longitude 0 degrees.

**Prominences** Masses of glowing hydrogen gas rising from the bright surface of the Sun.

**Proper motion, Stellar** The individual motion of a star on the celestial sphere.

**Proton** A fundamental particle with unit positive electrical charge.

**Pulsar** A rotating neutron star, emitting pulsed radio waves.

**Quadrature** The position of the Moon, planet or other body when at right angles to the Sun as seen from the Earth.

**Quasar** A very remote, super-luminous object; the nucleus of a very active galaxy.

**Radial velocity** The toward-or-away movement of a celestial body relative to the observer.

**Radiant** The point in the sky from which the meteors of any particular shower appear to diverge.

**Radius vector** A straight line between a fixed point and a variable point.

**Retardation** The difference in the time of moonrise from one night to the next.

**Retrograde motion** Orbital or rotational movement in a sense opposite to that of the Earth's axial or orbital rotation.

**Right ascension** The angular distance of a celestial body from the vernal equinox, measured eastward. It is usually given in units of time: the interval between the culmination of the vernal equinox, and the culmination of the object.

**Schmidt telescope** An instrument which collects its light by means of a spherical mirror; a correcting plate is placed at the top of the tube.

**Seyfert galaxies** Galaxies with relatively small, bright nuclei and weak spiral arms. Most of them are powerful radio emitters.

**Sidereal period** The revolution period of a planet or other body round the Sun, or of a satellite round a planet.

**Sidereal time** The local time reckoned according to the apparent rotation of the celestial sphere. When the vernal equinox crosses the observer's meridian, the sidereal time is 0 hours.

**Solar wind** A flow of particles streaming out constantly from the Sun.

**Solstices** The times when the Sun is at its maximum declination: $23\frac{1}{2}$ degrees north or south.

**Spectroscopic binary** A binary system whose components are too close together to be seen separately from Earth, but which can be tracked down by the Doppler shifts in their spectra.

**Speculum** The main mirror of a reflecting telescope.

**Superior planet** A planet whose orbit is further from the Sun than that of the Earth.

**Supernova** A colossal stellar outburst, involving (I) the destruction if the white dwarf component of a binary system, or (II) the collapse of a very massive star. A Type II supernova usually produces a neutron star, which emits pulsed radio waves and is termed a **Pulsar**.

**Synodic period** The interval between successive oppositions of a superior planet.

**Syzygy** The position of the Moon in its orbit when new or full.

**Tektites** Small, glassy objects found in restricted areas of the Earth. They are probably of terrestrial origin.

**Terminator** The boundary between the sunlit and night sides of the Moon or a planet.

**Transit** 1. The passage of a celestial body across the observer's meridian. 2. The passage of an inferior planet across the face of the Sun.

**Umbra** 1. The main cone of shadow cast by the Earth. 2. The darkest part of a sunspot.

**Van Allen Zones** Zones of charged particles surrounding the Earth.

**Variable stars** Stars which change in output over relatively short periods.

**White dwarf** A very small, dense, highly evolved star.

**Zenith** The observer's overhead point.

**Zodiac** The belt stretching round the sky, 8 degrees to either side of the ecliptic, in which the Sun, Moon and principal planets are always to be found.

**Zodiacal Light** A cone of light stretching upward from the horizon and extending along the ecliptic. It is due to sunlight illuminating interplanetary material in the main plane of the Solar System.

**Zürich number** A count of the sunspot activity. It is given by the formula $Z = k (10g + f)$, where $Z$ is the Zürich number, $g$ is the number of groups seen, $f$ is the number of individual spots, and $k$ is a constant depending on the observer's equipment; it is usually near 1. Zürich numbers are also known as Wolf numbers; the system was devised by R. Wolf of Zürich in 1852.

# — APPENDICES —

## Appendix 1 – Planetary Data

| Planet | Mean distance from Sun, millions of miles | Orbital Period | Axial Rotation period | Inclination of Axis degrees |
|---|---|---|---|---|
| Mercury | 36 | 88 days | 58.6 days | 2 |
| Venus | 67 | 224.7 days | 243 days | 178 |
| Earth | 93 | 365.2 days | 23h 56m | 23.4 |
| Mars | 141.5 | 687 days | 24h 37m | 24 |
| Jupiter | 483 | 11.9 years | 9h 50m | 3 |
| Saturn | 886 | 29.5 years | 10h 14m | 26 |
| Uranus | 1783 | 84 years | 17h 14m | 98 |
| Neptune | 2793 | 164.8 years | 16h 7m | 29 |
| Pluto | 3666 | 247.7 years | 6d 9h | 122 |

| Planet | Orbital eccentricity | Orbital inclination, degrees | Maximum mag. | No. of satellites |
|---|---|---|---|---|
| Mercury | 0.206 | 7.0 | –1.9 | 0 |
| Venus | 0.007 | 3.4 | –4.4 | 0 |
| Earth | 0.017 | 0 | – | 1 |
| Mars | 0.093 | 1.9 | –2.8 | 2 |
| Jupiter | 0.048 | 1.3 | –2.6 | 16 |
| Saturn | 0.056 | 2.5 | –0.3 | 18 |
| Uranus | 0.047 | 0.8 | +5.6 | 15 |
| Neptune | 0.009 | 1.8 | +7.7 | 8 |
| Pluto | 0.248 | 17.1 | +14 | 1 |

| Planet | Diameter, miles (equatorial) | Escape velocity miles/sec | Surface gravity, Earth = 1 | Mass, Earth = 1 | Mean surface temp, $^0C$ |
|---|---|---|---|---|---|
| Mercury | 3,030 | 2.6 | 0.38 | 0.06 | +427 |
| Venus | 7,523 | 6.4 | 0.90 | 0.86 | +480 |
| Earth | 7,926 | 7.0 | 1 | 1 | +22 |
| Mars | 4,222 | 3.2 | 0.38 | 0.11 | −23 |
| Jupiter | 89,424 | 37 | 2.64 | 318 | −150 |
| Saturn | 74,914 | 22 | 1.16 | 95 | −180 |
| Uranus | 31,770 | 14 | 1.17 | 15 | −214 |
| Neptune | 31,410 | 15 | 1.2 | 17 | −220 |
| Pluto | 1,444 | 0.7 | 0.06 | 0.002 | −230 |

# Appendix 2 –
# The Principal Planetary Satellites

Jupiter has 11 minor satellites. Metis, Adrastea and Thebe move within the orbit of Io, and the rest beyond the orbit of Callisto; Leda, Himalia, Lysithea and Elara form one group, and Ananke, Carme, Pasiphaë and Sinope the other. The last four have retrograde motion.

Saturn has 8 minor satellites: Pan, Atlas, Prometheus, Janus and Epimetheus move within the orbit of Mimas, and Telesto and Calypso are co-orbital with Tethys. Several more minor satellites have recently been suspected.

Uranus has ten minor satellites within the orbit of Miranda: Cordelia, Ophelia, Bianca, Cressida, Desdemona, Juliet, Portia, Rosalind, Belinda and Puck.

Neptune has six minor satellites moving within the orbit of Triton: Naiad, Thalassa, Despina, Galatea, Larissa and Proteus.

| Name | Mean distance from centre of primary, thousands of miles | Orbital Period d  h  m | Diameter miles (max) | Magnitude |
|---|---|---|---|---|
| | | EARTH | | |
| Moon | 239 | 27 7 43 | 2160 | −12.7 (full) |
| | | MARS | | |
| Phobos | 5.8 | 0  7 39 | 17 x 14 x 11 | 11.6 |
| Deimos | 14.6 | 1  6 18 | 9 x  7 x  6 | 12.8 |
| | | JUPITER | | |
| Amalthea | 113 | 0 11 57 | 163 x 91 x 89 | 14.1 |
| Io | 262 | 1 18 28 | 2264 | 5.0 |
| Europa | 417 | 3 13 14 | 1945 | 5.3 |
| Ganymede | 666 | 7  3 43 | 3274 | 4.6 |
| Callisto | 1170 | 16 16 32 | 2981 | 5.6 |
| | | SATURN | | |
| Mimas | 115 | 0 22 37 | 261 | 12.9 |
| Enceladus | 148 | 1  8 53 | 318 | 11.8 |
| Tethys | 183 | 1 21 18 | 650 | 10.3 |
| Dione | 235 | 2 17 41 | 696 | 10.4 |
| Rhea | 328 | 4 12 25 | 950 | 9.7 |
| Titan | 760 | 15 22 41 | 3201 | 8.3 |
| Hyperion | 920 | 21  6 38 | 224 | 14.2 |
| Iapetus | 2200 | 79  7 56 | 892 | 10var |
| Phoebe | 8050 | 550 10 50 | 143 | 16.5 |
| | | URANUS | | |
| Miranda | 81 | 1 19 50 | 293 | 16.5 |
| Ariel | 119 | 2 12 29 | 720 | 14.4 |
| Umbriel | 166 | 4  3 28 | 727 | 15.3 |
| Titania | 272 | 8 16 56 | 981 | 14.0 |
| Oberon | 365 | 13 11  7 | 947 | 14.2 |
| | | NEPTUNE | | |
| Triton | 220 | 5 21  3 | 1681 | 13.6 |
| Nereid | 3640 | 359 21  7 | 149 | 18.7 |
| | | PLUTO | | |
| Charon | 12.2 | 6  9 17 | 753 | 16.8 |

# Appendix 3 – Selected Asteroids

| | Mean distance from Sun, millions of miles | Orbital Period, years | Diameter, miles | Rotation period, hours | Magnitude |
|---|---|---|---|---|---|
| 1 Ceres | 257.0 | 4.61 | 584 | 9.1 | 7.4 |
| 2 Pallas | 257.4 | 4.62 | 360 x 292 | 7.8 | 8.0 |
| 3 Juno | 247.8 | 4.36 | 179 x 143 | 7.2 | 8.7 |
| 4 Vesta | 219.3 | 3.63 | 358 | 5.3 | 6.5 |
| 5 Astrae | 239.3 | 4.14 | 75 | 16.8 | 9.8 |
| 10 Hygeia | 292.6 | 5.59 | 267 | 17.5 | 10.2 |
| 243 Ida | 260.4 | 4.84 | 24 x 21 | 4.6 | 14.6 |
| 279 Thule | 394.8 | 8.23 | 81 | | 15.4 |
| 433 Eros | 166.9 | 1.76 | 15 | 5.3 | 8.6 (max) |
| 588 Achilles | 470 | 11.77 | 72 | 58 | 15.3 |
| 944 Hidalgo | 365 | 14.15 | 17 | 10 | 15.3 |
| 951 Gaspra | 187 | 3.28 | 15 | 20 | 14.1 |
| 1221 Amor | 140 | 2.66 | 1 | | 18 |
| 1566 Icarus | 120 | 1.12 | 1 | 2.3 | 18 |
| 1685 Toro | 99 | 1.60 | 5 | 7.6 | 10.2 |
| 1862 Apollo | 99 | 1.78 | 1 | 1.4 | 17 |
| 2060 Chiron | 1255 | 50.7 | 150 | 6 | 17 |
| 2062 Aten | 81 | 0.95 | 1 | | 18 |
| 2100 Ra-Shalom | 61 | 0.76 | 0.3 | 20 | 19 |
| 2340 Hathor | 61 | 0.77 | 0.3 | | 19 |
| 3200 Phaethon | 66 | 1.43 | 3 | 4 | 17 |
| 5145 Pholus | 1893 | 93 | 150 | | 21 |
| 1992 QB1 | 3100 | 290 | 150 | | 21 |

# Appendix 4 – Selected Comets

| Name | Period, Years | Distance from Sun, millions of miles: | |
| --- | --- | --- | --- |
| | | min | max |
| Encke | 3.3 | 32 | 380 |
| Grigg–Skjellerup | 5.1 | 93 | 460 |
| D' Arrest | 6.2 | 110 | 520 |
| Pons–Winnecke | 6.3 | 116 | 520 |
| Giacobini–Zinner | 6.5 | 92 | 550 |
| Finlay | 6.9 | 102 | 580 |
| Faye | 7.4 | 150 | 560 |
| Tuttle | 13.3 | 95 | 970 |
| Crommelin | 27.9 | 69 | 1640 |
| Tempel–Tuttle | 32.9 | 91 | 1820 |
| Halley | 76.1 | 55 | 3290 |
| Swift–Tuttle | 130 | 89 | 4800 |

## Principal Meteor Showers

| Name | Begins | Max | Ends | ZHR |
| --- | --- | --- | --- | --- |
| Quadrantids | 1 Jan | 4 Jan | 6 Jan | 60 |
| Lyrids | 19 Apr | 21 Apr | 25 Apr | 10 |
| Perseids | 23 July | 12 Aug | 20 Aug | 75 |
| Orionids | 16 Oct | 22 Oct | 27 Oct | 25 |
| Taurids | 20 Oct | 3 Nov | 30 Nov | 10 |
| Leonids | 15 Nov | 17 Nov | 20 Nov | var. |
| Geminids | 7 Dec | 13 Dec | 16 Dec | 75 |

# Appendix 5 – The Constellations

Large and important constellations are given in capital letters. Hemisphere indicates the position of the main part of the constellation. Z indicates Zodiacal.

| Name | English name star(s) | 1st-mag. | Hemisphere |
|---|---|---|---|
| ANDROMEDA | Andromeda | – | N |
| Antlia | The Air-pump | – | S |
| Apus | The Bird of Paradise | – | S |
| AQUARIUS | The Water-bearer | – | S Z |
| AQUILA | The Eagle | Altair | N |
| Ara | The Altar | – | S |
| ARIES | The Ram | – | N Z |
| AURIGA | The Charioteer | Capella | N |
| BOÖTES | The Herdsman | Arcturus | N |
| Caelum | The Graving Tool | – | S |
| Camelopardalis | The Giraffe | – | N |
| CANCER | The Crab | – | N Z |
| Canes Venatici | The Hunting Dogs | – | N |
| CANIS MAJOR | The Great Dog | Sirius | S |
| Canis Minor | The Little Dog | Procyon | N |
| CAPRICORNUS | The Sea-Goat | – | S Z |
| CARINA | The Keel | Canopus | S |
| CASSIOPEIA | Cassiopeia | – | N |
| CENTAURUS | The Centaur | Alpha Centauri, Agena | S |
| Cepheus | Cepheus | – | N |
| CETUS | The Whale | – | S |
| Chamaeleon | The Chameleon | – | S |
| Circinus | The Compasses | – | S |
| Columba | The Dove | – | S |
| Coma Berenices | Berenice's Hair | – | N |
| Corona Australis | The Southern Crown | – | S |
| Corona Borealis | The Northern Crown | – | N |
| Corvus | The Crow | – | S |
| Crater | The Cup | – | S |
| CRUX AUSTRALIS | The Southern Cross | Acrux, Beta Crucis | S |

| | | | |
|---|---|---|---|
| CYGNUS | The Swan | Deneb | N |
| Delphinus | The Dolphin | – | N |
| Dorado | The Swordfish | – | S |
| DRACO | The Dragon | – | N |
| Equuleus | The Foal | – | N |
| ERIDANUS | The River | Achernar | S |
| Fornax | The Furnace | – | S |
| GEMINI | The Twins | Pollux | N |
| Grus | The Crane | – | S |
| HERCULES | Hercules | – | N |
| Horologium | The Clock | – | S |
| HYDRA | The Watersnake | – | S |
| Hydrus | The Little Snake | – | S |
| Indus | The Indian | – | S |
| Lacerta | The Lizard | – | N |
| LEO | The Lion | Regulus | N |
| Leo Minor | The Little Lion | – | N |
| Lepus | The Hare | – | S |
| LIBRA | The Balance | – | S Z |
| Lupus | The Wolf | – | S |
| Lynx | The Lynx | – | N |
| LYRA | The Lyre | Vega | N |
| Mensa | The Table | – | S |
| Microscopium | The Microscope | – | S |
| Monoceros | The Unicorn | – | Equatorial |
| Musca Australis | The Southern Fly | – | S |
| Norma | The Rule | – | S |
| Octans | The Octant | – | S |
| OPHIUCHUS | The Serpent-bearer | – | Equatorial |
| ORION | Orion | Rigel, Betelgeux | Equatorial |
| Pavo | The Peacock | – | S |
| PEGASUS | The Flying Horse | – | N |
| PERSEUS | Perseus | – | N |
| Phoenix | The Phoenix | – | S |
| Pictor | The Painter | – | S |
| Pisces | The Fishes | – | N Z |
| Piscis Australis | The Southern Fish | Fomalhaut | S |
| PUPPIS | The Poop | – | S |
| Pyxis | The Mariner's Compass | – | S |

| | | | |
|---|---|---|---|
| Reticulum | The Net | – | S |
| Sagitta | The Arrow | – | N |
| SAGITTARIUS | The Archer | – | S Z |
| SCORPIUS | The Scorpion | Antares | S Z |
| Sculptor | The Sculptor | – | S |
| Scutum | The Shield | – | S |
| Serpens | The Serpent | – | N |
| Sextans | The Sextant | – | S |
| TAURUS | The Bull | Aldebaran | N |
| Telescopium | The Telescope | – | S |
| Triangulum | The Triangle | – | N |
| Triangulum Australe | The Southern Triangle | – | S |
| Tucana | The Toucan | – | S |
| URSA MAJOR | The Great Bear | – | N |
| URSA MINOR | The Little Bear | – | N |
| VELA | The Sails | – | S |
| VIRGO | The Virgin | Spica | Equatorial |
| Volans | The Flying Fish | – | S |
| Vulpecula | The Fox | – | N |

# Appendix 6 –
# Stars of the First Magnitude

| | | Spectrum | Magnitude | Declination ° |
|---|---|---|---|---|
| Alpha Canis Majoris | Sirius | A | −1.5 | −17 |
| Alpha Carinae | Canopus | F | −0.7 | −53 |
| Alpha Centauri | | K+G | −0.3 | −61 |
| Alpha Boötis | Arcturus | K | −0.0 | +19 |
| Alpha Lyrae | Vega | A | 0.0 | +39 |
| Alpha Aurigae | Capella | G | 0.1 | +46 |
| Beta Orionis | Rigel | B | 0.1 | −08 |
| Alpha Canis Minoris | Procyon | F | 0.4 | +02 |
| Alpha Eridani | Achernar | B | 0.5 | −57 |
| Alpha Orionis | Betelgeux | M | var. | +07 |
| Beta Centauri | Agena | B | 0.6 | −60 |
| Alpha Aquilae | Altair | A | 0.8 | +09 |
| Alpha Crucis | Acrux | B+B | 0.8 | −63 |
| Alpha Tauri | Aldebaran | K | 0.8 | +17 |
| Alpha Scorpii | Antares | M | 1.0 | −26 |
| Alpha Virginis | Spica | B | 1.0 | −11 |
| Beta Geminorum | Pollux | K | 1.1 | +28 |
| Alpha Piscis Australis | Fomalhaut | A | 1.2 | −30 |
| Alpha Cygni | Deneb | A | 1.2 | +45 |
| Beta Crucis | | B | 1.2 | −60 |
| Alpha Leonis | Regulus | B | 1.3 | +12 |

Next in order come Epsilon Canis Majoris (1.5), and Alpha Geminorum (Castor), Gamma Crucis, Lambda Scorpii, Gamma Orionis and Beta Tauri (all 1.6).

# Appendix 7 –
# Proper Names of Stars

Very few stars below the first magnitude have proper names which are in general use, but the following are found often enough to be worth listing here.

| | |
|---|---|
| Alpha Andromedae | Alpheratz |
| Epsilon Boötis | Izar |
| Alpha Canum Venaticorum | Cor Caroli |
| Epsilon Canis Majoris | Adhara |
| Alpha Cassiopeiae | Shedir |
| Beta Ceti | Diphda |
| Omicron Ceti | Mira |
| Alpha Coronae Borealis | Alphekka |
| Beta Cygni | Albireo |
| Alpha Draconis | Thuban |
| Theta Eridani | Acamar |
| Alpha Geminorum | Castor |
| Gamma Geminorum | Alhena |
| Alpha Herculis | Rasalgethi |
| Alpha Hydrae | Alphard |
| Beta Leonis | Denebola |
| Gamma Leonis | Algieba |
| Alpha Ophiuchi | Rasalhague |
| Gamma Orionis | Bellatrix |
| Delta Orionis | Mintaka |
| Epsilon Orionis | Alnilam |
| Zeta Orionis | Alnitak |
| Kappa Orionis | Saiph |
| Beta Pegasi | Scheat |
| Alpha Persei | Mirphak |
| Beta Persei | Algol |
| Lambda Scorpii | Shaula |
| Upsilon Scorpii | Lesath |
| Beta Tauri | Alnath |
| Eta Tauri | Alcyone |
| Alpha Ursae Majoris | Dubhe |
| Beta Ursae Majoris | Merak |

| | |
|---|---|
| Gamma Ursae Majoris | Phad |
| Delta Ursae Majoris | Megrez |
| Epsilon Ursae Majoris | Alioth |
| Zeta Ursae Majoris | Mizar |
| Eta Ursae Majoris | Alkaid |
| 80 Ursae Majoris | Alcor |
| Alpha Ursae Minoris | Polaris |
| Beta Ursae Minoris | Kocab |

# INDEX